395
/2N

AD

31
U

The School and the Democratic Environment

PAPERS AND OTHER MATERIALS
DRAWN FROM A CONFERENCE SPONSORED BY THE
DANFORTH FOUNDATION AND THE FORD FOUNDATION

THE DANFORTH FOUNDATION
& THE FORD FOUNDATION

THE SCHOOL
AND THE
DEMOCRATIC
ENVIRONMENT

COLUMBIA UNIVERSITY PRESS

1970 *New York and London*

FOREWORD

In April, 1969, the Danforth and Ford Foundations sponsored a conference in Washington, D.C., on "The School and the Democratic Environment." The purpose of the conference was to explore how the schools can better prepare young people to function in a democratic society beset by unprecedented demands and complexity. Since the times of ancient Greece, the educational system has been expected to transmit society's basic political and social values to the young, thus preserving stability and consensus in the adult population. But in the United States today, stability and consensus are conspicuously lacking; there is strong, open conflict between the dominant society and ethnic groups, between the affluent and the poor, between the young and the not so young. Obviously, then, citizenship education in this country has been less than successful.

The kind of education that is needed is one that prepares the youth of this nation intellectually, psychologically, and politically to be active citizens in the decades ahead. Inculcating them with a blind allegiance to our system is not only undesirable but quite likely impossible given the nature and intelligence of students, particularly today's students. Furthermore, a reliance on the platitudes about American society may do more harm than good. In class, students hear and read about America the beautiful—and what they hear about *is* beautiful—but when they look around them what they see is sometimes ugly: war, racial injustice, poverty. And what they do learn from school practices is often a conscious or unconscious denial of the participation, liberty, equality, and justice theories they heard about in civics class. Students hear about libertarian precepts, but they see and experience authoritarian treatment. Such differences between theory and reality only feed student unrest.

The conference was not specifically intended to delve into the problem of student unrest in the schools since student rebels may be more symptomatic of what is wrong with the schools than the ill itself. Students, of course, were not the first to point out the faults of the school systems; educators like John Holt have been saying the same things for a lot longer. But the student actions—many of them less than responsible—have been dramatic, and because students seem to be louder than most educators, they are apparently succeeding where others have failed in focusing much needed attention on the schools and what is wrong with them.

The months preceding the conference had seen junior high and high school students intensifying their efforts to force the schools to meet their demands (some of the more responsible ones being relevant education, the extension of the rights of citizenship to students, and the end to racial injustice). The students—perhaps taking a lesson from their older brothers and sisters in college—had increasingly turned to stronger tactics to gain their goals. Serious disruptions in the schools increased, and, by the end of the school year, an estimated 6,000 such disturbances had occurred. Consequently, no conference participant could overlook the student rebels.

But authoritarian schools affect more than just the students. They create a climate that stifles teachers, as well, and everyone else who comes in contact with the schools. And just as the question of authoritarian schools is bigger than the students, so, too, is citizenship education more than just the problem of the schools. The school is a microcosm of the community. It is not a leader in the change process; it mirrors the community's feelings. If the community cannot agree on the desirability of a more articulated role for the schools in the political socialization of its young, then school executives, school boards, administrators, and teachers, in all likelihood, will feel little pressure to take positive steps to correct present imbalances and failings.

Since educators alone will never decide how citizenship education will be handled in the schools, the Danforth-Ford conference broadened the usual discussion of the schools' problems by including a diverse group of Federal officials, civic leaders, and professional men and women as well as educators. (For a list of participants invited to the conference, see page 109.) Yet this group of people could no more find the answers than could any other group. That was not the meeting's intention. Its purpose was simply to extend the dialogue among these people with their varied interests and concerns that could eventually filter down into local communities to serve as a basis for school reform. It was successful in extending the dialogue, but no single meeting or short period of time can bring about school reform.

Since the conference was held, however, some changes have taken place. First, important educators, like U.S. Commissioner of Education James Allen and H.E.W. Secretary Robert H. Finch, have increasingly stated their support for many of the demands, if not the actions, of the students and others associated with schools who are protesting the way the schools are run.

In September, Commissioner Allen said, "One of my assistants summed it up by saying, 'If you feel student unrest is a problem rather than a manifestation of root problems within our society—then you are a part of the problem.' I do not suggest here that violence and destruction can be condoned. It must be firmly dealt with in terms of the laws that apply. But a repressive approach is a simplistic approach, one that could do far more harm than good. We need, instead, to look, to listen, and to learn more about what underlies the growing unrest."

The Secretary and Commissioner went one step beyond the talk stage this fall when the Office of Education and the Department of Health, Education and Welfare set up a Task Force on Students and Social Change to help bring about a climate in which needed educational changes can take place and make the department more responsive to student needs.

Second, on the local level, principals and administrators have begun to meet with students to discuss their concerns. This communication is a beginning, but it cannot, in and of itself, be the solution. In addition, more and more parents, particularly those of black and middle-class white students, have begun to support many of their children's more justified goals.

Third, the number of incidents involving student demands for change has increased (3,500 during the first three months of the 1969-70 school year), but the violence has decreased. There are a number of reasons for the decrease in violence. The radical movement has splintered into factions, and more radical students have angered the less violent. Furthermore, many students have turned their efforts toward ending the war in Vietnam and have little time for the high school movement. Administrators have clearly indicated when they will call out the police or invoke court orders, thus removing any ambiguity about that question. Additionally, some school systems (for example, New York City and the state of New Jersey) have drawn up bills of rights for students—rights that were once either ignored or subject to whim or capricious interpretations by school administrators.

However, the lessening of violence does not mean that the student movement is weakening. The increase in the number of incidents attests to that. Few schools will escape the turmoil. Few communities will avoid having to decide how they will handle their student rebels—whether they will only try to "cool it" by dealing with surface problems or whether they will attempt to channel this unrest into constructive efforts toward more perfect schools.

The Danforth and Ford Foundations have made several grants—for efforts ranging from curricular reform to attempts to overcome interracial and intergenerational tensions—at helping to move the schools in the direction of better, more relevant education. The Danforth-Ford conference was one of these efforts. Perhaps the papers summarized here will be valuable, as they were at the conference, in extending the dialogue in large and small school districts throughout the country that will lead to a more democratic environment in which students can learn. It is, after all, the responsibility of the schools to prepare young people to be active citizens.

Dr. Gene L. Schwilck
Vice President, The Danforth Foundation

Dr. Edward J. Meade, Jr.
Program Officer in Charge,
Public Education, The Ford Foundation

CONTENTS

Introduction

Marvin R. Weisbord

WHAT DO WE WANT FROM OUR SCHOOLS?

WANTING TO "DO" something about all problems, right
now, seems a peculiarly American trait. What to do,
in fact, rivals baseball as a national pastime. Nowhere
is this more evident than in regard to public schools.
Education, the universal equalizer, our only inescapable
institution, engages about 65 million of us—nearly one-
third of the population of the United States.

Practically everybody, then, would like to "do" something about schools or, put another way, have the
schools "do" something about everything—physical,
social, cultural, intellectual, and economic. Above all,
everybody wants the schools to produce good citizens.
Whatever other tasks we impose, citizenship education
—the production of informed, useful, concerned, loyal
Americans—has always been the school's unique responsibility. There is no public board of education in
the United States that would not defend the "statement
of philosophy" of a Midwest high school which begins,

MARVIN R. WEISBORD, journalist, acted as official observer at the
Danforth-Ford conference.

"We believe that the function of the public school is to preserve the democratic ideal by educating each individual for effective participation in democracy."

How successful schools are in this aim is called into question by an unprecedented wave of unrest sweeping American high schools. A 1969 survey, done, interestingly, by the "establishment," for example, showed two-thirds of city and suburban and more than half of rural schools reporting serious student disruptions, and, in one principal's words, "we're just getting started on this protest business." His contention is borne out by the hundreds of incidents Dr. Alan Westin cites in his speech (see pages 65-82), and by such articles as "Strategies for Coping with Boycotts, Violence, and Sit-Ins," which appeared in a recent issue of *School Management* magazine. This is capped by the focus of Harvard University's 1969 Advanced Administrative Institute for school executives entirely on "The Youth Revolution."

Student unrest, especially where it has been violent or destructive, suggests that many schools have failed —despite patriotic songs, flag salutes, stories of heroism, holiday celebrations, student governments, or civics lessons—"to preserve the democratic ideal" among a growing number of young people. The issues students raise—race, censorship, free speech, dress codes, discipline, course content—affect not only their lives in school but their attitudes, ultimately, as citizens. Student protest provokes serious questions about freedom, justice, authority, responsibility, order, rights, stability—the crucial abstractions around which society is built.

But students are not the only protesters. In many

places, parents, too, dissatisfied with what they see as low-quality education, have organized to influence schools in ways other than through school board meetings. Taxpayers, reluctant to part with more money as student unrest and racial tensions increase, have voted down bond issues necessary to keep public schools operating. Free public education stands in serious jeopardy from various persons practicing what they conceive to be "effective participation in democracy" in ways not taught in schools.

To open a national discussion of what the schools' citizenship role ought to be in this rapidly changing society, the Ford and Danforth Foundations last April invited more than 100 diverse civic organizations— from the American Legion to the National Association for the Advancement of Colored People, from the American Federation of Teachers to the Daughters of the American Revolution, from the Chamber of Commerce to the Girl Scouts of America—to confer in Washington, D.C. This unusual forum united teachers, businessmen, doctors, lawyers, ministers, school executives, social workers, government officials—some conservative, some radical, some militant, some hesitant— in a common search for the many problems underlying the relationship between "the school and the democratic environment."

Using papers, films, panel discussions, and demonstration classes, the participants raised questions about schools which are rarely discussed outside the circle of professional educators. Most of those attending felt somehow stimulated and enlightened by this critical look at education. Yet many expressed frustration at the lack of "answers" that emerged. Three days of

intense interaction simply highlighted how difficult it
is to pinpoint the various issues, let alone prescribe
what people should "do" about them.

What, for example, are schools "really like"? A conference film (see pages 55-64) from the students'
viewpoint was assembled from movies made in various
schools across the continent. The composite picture
was of a stifling institution, where children walk in
military file, keep their mouths shut, tell teachers what
they want to hear, and generally sacrifice creativity,
growth, and involvement to a sort of mindless pressure
for order and conformity. The film generated great
emotion, first a silence that hung like smog over the
audience, then an hour of heated discussion among the
conferees. Yet few would agree whether it was a fair
portrayal of what goes on in schools.

"It's one-sided," said a gray-haired law enforcement
official. "I don't believe schools are really that bad." To
which a lady in a flowered hat replied, "I've been teaching in high schools for twenty years, and I want to
throw up. I'm sorry, sir, but that's just the way it is."
And yet, in fairness to the law officer, one must acknowledge there are many "good things" about schools
which the film did not portray, including sensitive,
humane teachers, like the lady in the flowered hat,
who wish as fervently as the students that things might
be different.

Unending disagreements over facts, issues, analyses,
priorities, marked the conference. Some saw race conflict as the overriding issue in school and society. Others
saw it as the larger question of whether or not what we
call education is any longer useful to anybody, whatever his color, in a world which seems to make itself

obsolete every ten years. Many argued a line heard
more and more among social scientists—"you can't
teach democracy in a dictatorship." The emphasis in
schools on order defeats educational aims.

Observing the problem of schools in democracy, as
it emerged at the Danforth-Ford conference, was like
looking into a kaleidoscope. The pattern changed with
each speaker. Yet the issues, like the bits of colored
glass, seemed inseparable, no matter how they were
arranged. It seems futile to discuss the schools' citizenship role without raising such complex questions as
What is worth learning at all? How do schools respond
to conflict? What constitutes good human relations?
and so on. Schools, the conference made clear, consti-
tute a system—an intricate set of assumptions, relationships, and practices, which vary together.

Yet each of us, depending on his job, his viewpoint,
his experience, picks out a piece of the puzzle as his
priority. It is no surprise that some conference participants felt cheated at hearing issues raised (i.e.,
ghetto schools, poverty) which they felt were outside
the discussion's scope at the same time those raising
the issues felt they were the only legitimate ones.

No wonder then that the desire for closure, for a
specific action program, could not be met. What to do
about civic education remains an open question. It
cannot be otherwise, given the diversity of opinions
and the complexity of the issues. The prior task must
be to see whether some common understandings about
schools can be arrived at.

Through the papers and speeches printed here,
through the heated arguments in the conference, run
two overriding themes which require extended and

serious discussion. Any news account of student dissent reveals concern with one or the other, and more
often both. Since it is widespread student dissent that
has forced this critical look at schools, let us consider
these two themes first from the students' point of view.
Here is what they say:

1. We want learning to be exciting, alive, related
to our own feelings and problems and to the important
issues that shape the world we will inherit, whether
war, race, sex, drugs, life styles, or ways of getting a
living.

2. We want to be treated with respect and credited
with the same needs for status, influence, power,
achievement, and feelings of self-worth that principals,
teachers, or parents have, despite any differences in age
or values.

The first issue concerns curricula and teaching
styles, and the subject matter appropriate to education. The second has to do with the management of
education—the pattern of policies, decisions, rules, rewards, punishments, and exercise of power in schools.
Let us consider each in more detail.

First, Is there a contradiction between school work
(what is taught) and students' needs, feelings, goals,
and perceptions of the world around them (what is
learned)? No parent can fail to recognize the extraor-
dinary changes for the better that have taken place
in the teaching of math and science in the past decade.
But the social studies, which deal most intimately with
human interaction in society, have changed very little.
In recent years study after study—of textbooks, course
materials, student attitudes—reveals that many schools
serve up at best a platitudinous view of society, and a

downright false and ultimately disillusioning one at worst.

Far from turning out good citizens, there is much evidence that the textbook view of democracy contributes to student cynicism and unrest. Texts make naïve statements about democracy, citing the vote as the supreme political act, ignoring conflict, controversy, or unpleasantness. Former Vice President Hubert Humphrey made the point forcefully in a radio interview when he commented that he wished he could give his erstwhile students their money back. "What I taught them about government and politics had little to do with what I learned when I became Mayor and later a U.S. Senator," he said.

Furthermore, most schools emphasize what appear to be blind loyalty and mindless patriotism without acknowledging the diverse interpretations Americans put on these attitudes. To take the simplest example, many citizens believe it is the highest form of patriotism to support the war in Vietnam, while others feel with equal fervor that it is the duty of every citizen to oppose it. Schools, rather than air these conflicting views, tend to duck the issue, and with good reason. Prowar and antiwar parents alike resist having their children exposed to the other side's "propaganda" in school.

The same holds true for many controversial issues, sex education, for example, which has polarized parents and teachers across the country. Perhaps, unlike the students, we prefer to air conflict issues in letters-to-the-editor, on radio talk shows, and in acrimonious school-board meetings, instead of permitting them to become the subject of mature discussion in school. If that is the case, why should educators, always under pressure from some quarter, make paradoxical, unresolved, and emotionally charged social issues the substance of classroom talk? Do we want students exposed to the pros and cons of race conflict, war, premarital sex, or censorship as part of education? Or must school, so as not to offend anybody, always be based on a set of relatively neutral "facts"?

Suburban students especially, many of them college bound, vigorously challenge the value of factual knowledge. The notion that all questions have right or wrong answers, which they know is false, offends them. Increasingly students resist studying simply to pass college entrance exams. They argue that learning ought to mean personal growth and involvement, not a constant round of passing tests and making grades. Given the alternative, few reject college outright. But they see the treadmill paradox of always studying not for the joy of knowledge but to reach another plateau, where new facts to be memorized await them.

In the words of college psychiatrist Seymour L. Halleck, "They tend to see education as an end in itself, something to be enjoyed, even worshipped as a noble activity of man." Against this value, then, they deplore competition for grades, the traditional motivator for generations of students. They hold in contempt the teacher who uses homework as punishment and rewards students by excusing them from study. Even those who believe learning should be fun and feel uneasy about grade competition recognize that some tangible reward structure is necessary for effective learning today.

Can we devise reward systems in school to foster

growth and involvement in education? Can we learn how to measure progress in new ways? Unfortunately, these are not questions any one school or principal or teacher or even board can act on alone. Education's measurement and reward structure grows out of a complex social system, starting with college admission standards, which affect even preschool education, locked into state laws and accrediting procedures, and frozen in tradition. To move away from fact-bound, memorized knowledge into reasoning, problem-solving, theorizing, where right and wrong answers matter less than the quality of understanding, requires a significant revision in the way we measure educational progress.

Hence the question of relevant studies cannot be considered without looking at the structure of rewards. Some individual teachers and a few schools experiment with pass-fail grading, or peer-grading, or self-grading, but nobody has hit on a perfect system. Somehow, the door to more experimentation must be opened. This is a hard thing to do so long as comparable standards—a student's "record"—remains the ticket of admission to jobs or college.

Black ghetto students also raise the question of education's relevance to their lives and futures, but few enjoy the luxury of asking whether what they study is the best route to college. Black students, and increasingly Mexican-American and the American Indian students, want recognition of their unique origins and identities. This implies special courses in ethnic history and sociology, not just so they will know more about themselves but as a symbol that society—and the school in particular—acknowledges that they matter.

Moreover, they want the school to accept some responsibility for preparing them for the future with job skills and a realistic understanding of opportunities in a changing world. Above all, like their suburban peers, they want some control and influence over their environment. All students, everywhere, care very much about the quality of life in school. They passionately resist rules, orders, decisions, policies which strike them as arbitrary, unfair, or punitive. So powerful is this drive among students that it transcends race conflict in many schools.

As one student leader in a California high school told an interviewer, "In the morning we had been fighting. But by the end of that meeting we were standing together against the principal. In just a couple of hours we were back together, unified in one student body. And that's the way it is now. And it's going to be white and black, green, purple, all different colored people fighting against him and his administration."

"Him and his administration." Ultimately, any talk about education comes around to the way the school itself is organized. Where do the rules and practices which govern daily life in school come from? What purposes do they serve? Some bold educators suggest that the school's own pattern of operation, and student dissent from it, should *be* the social studies curriculum, that students are highly motivated to understand citizenship issues which affect them directly (just as their parents or teachers are). Details change, but the issues —power, authority, responsibility, justice, and so on— remain the same, in or out of school.

This raises the second overriding question we must ask about education. Is there a contradiction between what schools preach about democracy—the platitudes of participation, critical thinking, respect for individuals—and what they actually practice in the halls, lunchrooms, and classes? Certainly schools vary enormously in how punitive or repressive they tend to be, depending often upon the personality of the principal. Yet no one can read Marker and Mehlinger's clinical description of school culture (see pages 38-54) without asking whether this is really what we want from schools. Few adults would permit any organization— company, professional, social, or government—to impose the kind of control on their lives which some schools presume it is their right, if not duty, to exercise.

"School systems," one young man tells his suburban school board, in a film clip shown at the conference, "make a real, concrete difference between human beings and students. The student doesn't have the right to analyze the school, to criticize the school beyond a few very limited areas. If he does, he's told by all the 'human beings' in the system that he's doing something very wrong."

This issue is enormously complicated by public education laws. Education may be free in America, but nobody is free to refuse to be educated. It is the inevitable fate of every citizen, whether he likes it or not. A business can choose its employees, and vice versa. But public schools and students, for better or worse, are stuck with each other.

The first paradox of a democratic school, then, is the premise that before anybody can be educated he must become an inmate. Schools have elaborate mechanisms for bringing everybody into the building and making sure they stay there the required number of days a year. From this constraint alone flows a stream of rules, policies, and paperwork—from seat assignments, to the taking of attendance, the checking of notes from parents and doctors, the filling out of forms—which require an inordinate amount of time. No wonder so many teachers, let alone students, feel harassed by practices they perceive as far removed from education. And this is just one example.

Moreover, nobody likes coercion, even in a good cause. We are compelled to admit that much of what we call education is inescapably unpleasant simply because it is inescapable. Having forced students into school in far greater numbers than the building was designed to accommodate, we are faced with the impossible task of creating an educational "climate," when from the start the whole operation smacks of confinement.

Forced to exercise control, fearful of losing it, school staffs create a complex web of don'ts, what the students call "No, No"s, which make up the fabric of school life: keep quiet, show your pass, raise your hand, don't chew gum, cut your hair, change your clothes, and above all, ask no questions about whether these rules are right, proper, effective, or necessary. Obviously this is not true of every school or every principal or every teacher. But the fact remains that the way education is organized, the way most students experience school and come to accept it, the way law and custom combine, make it possible for repressive practices—invasion of privacy, unfair punishment, threats, harassment—to be carried out by some teachers and administrators, no matter how many other sensitive, humane, kindly adults may also be present in the school.

Humanity, then, is not institutionalized in schools. It is talked about, but it is not a value built into the structure of the rules, policies, and practices. It occurs as a quirk of personality, which, fortunately, many school staff members have. But it is not required, universally practiced, or rewarded. Many people believe that a rigid emphasis on order, quiet, and routine is essential to the operation of schools, given the diversity of students, the many conflicts existing just below the surface, and the fear that students may "get out of control."

Indeed, everybody knows from experience that some students act badly in school, continually defying authority, disrupting classes, fighting, and hence must be sat upon all the time. Others argue that students disrupt because the work bores them and that repressive control sets up a self-fulfilling prophecy. Of course, schools are not laboratories, and it is very difficult to test this proposition in a scientific way. One way to test it, however, is with a leap of imagination. Imagine that schools, like businesses, had to compete for students, that those which could not attract and hold a large student body would fail, and the teachers, principals, and school-board members would lose their jobs. What then would schools look like?

What then would become of school executives who believe that the only way to run a school is to be personally responsible for, and controlling of, the behavior of every other person there? Obviously student appeals for alternatives to people who believe there are none inevitably fall on deaf ears. In consequence, students turn more and more to a higher authority—the courts—for relief from what they define as the school's violation of their citizenship rights. It will be years before a pattern of case decisions establishes whether or not students, despite forced attendance, enjoy full protection of the Bill of Rights. But some recent court decisions suggest that is the way the wind blows, and it can have serious implications for the management of schools. Last year, for example, Iowa students filed suit when principals refused to let them wear black armbands to symbolize their objection to the war in Vietnam. The U.S. Supreme Court, in a landmark decision, affirmed for the first time that school children have the same rights of free speech under the First Amendment to the Constitution as adults do. If they are not disruptive, they may express their political and social views during school hours.

In Wisconsin a Federal judge ordered a high school to reinstate a pupil suspended for wearing long hair. "It is time," wrote the judge, "to broaden the Constitutional community by including within its protection younger people whose claim to dignity matches that of their elders."

Court cases, together with boycotts, sit-ins, and violence seem oddly reminiscent of the labor-management disputes in the early days of the union movement. Again one must ask: Is this what we want from education? Must schools permanently play the role of antagonists to the interests of the people they were set up to serve?

One writer, Peter Schrag, suggests we may have no choice. "It is worth noting," he commented recently, "that repression has been part of every civilization, and that so far no educational system has been devised to make it obsolescent. Social order presumably depends on certain shared values and assumptions which do not necessarily grow from a context of totally free, open-ended inquiry."

Does this mean that it is impossible to design a public educational environment compatible with learning? Are we in fact prisoners of some human need that makes diversity of belief and tolerance for conflict nice abstractions but inappropriate to running schools? Many of us, it is true, given our own experience, see total anarchy as the only alternative to rigid control. Many students share this assumption. Not surprisingly, they opt for anarchy because, having been exposed to structures they see as bad, they conclude the fault lies with the idea of structure itself.

Few of us have experienced a "loose structure," one which has rules, responsibilities, rewards, and punishments yet is not repressive or antagonistic. Can we create "looser" public schools, in which principals share power without abdicating it, and in the process spread the responsibility for a stable school onto many shoulders? Can we conceive new ways to look at dissent, censorship, personal appearance, as educational issues, open-ended, not finite but as worthy of discussion in the classroom as in court? Or is the drive for conformity in public schools—based on parental pressure, group tensions, lack of goals, our inability to measure educational success—so profound that nothing can be done about it?

The twin problems—what schools ought to teach, and how they should be organized and managed—do not lend themselves to blanket statements. We need to

encourage new experiments in both areas. Indeed, we
need to encourage each state, each system, each board,
each school, each PTA to undertake an honest self-
examination. What should education be like? Is there
an anomaly between what students experience as life
in school and society and the formal education they
receive?

   If so, what should we do about it? If not, then why
do so many students see school as such an unfriendly
place?

Raising the Issues

Robert H. Finch

THAT QUESTION OF RELEVANCY

IN ANY PERIOD of explosive social change, established institutions come under concerted, bitter attack. Our age is no exception. The attack at times even questions whether any institutions at all, as we conceive them, are desirable to advance the human cause. The "code word" embodying that assault, and the transition to the new epoch, is "relevance."

We are told, for example, that the institutions along our entire educational spectrum, from Head Start through the graduate disciplines, are "irrelevant." Perhaps they are, in any number of possible ways. But analysis of the accusation demands a context. For the proper question is surely "irrelevant *with respect to what?*" Stated in that form, the question goes to the heart of our continuing social crisis, to the basic business of our educational institutions, and to the relationship of schools to the democratic environment.

Several generations ago, we turned to the public

THE HONORABLE ROBERT H. FINCH is Secretary of the Health, Education and Welfare Department.

schools to introduce new immigrants to the American way. We turned to the schools when we woke up one morning a decade ago to find a Russian satellite circling the globe. And we always turn to the schools when we need trained persons to fill our manpower needs.

In short, we turn to the schools to equip our society with the capability of coping with whatever it perceives to be its most urgent tasks. We turn to the public educational system—still one of the most radical ideas in human history—as the indispensable instrument of social change.

So we are turning to the schools again today to provide our growing generation with the tools to master the challenges of an increasingly complex technological society. And we put on the schools the principal burden of beating new paths to individual fulfillment, of making the promise of America an avenue broad enough for all to travel.

My predecessor John Gardner, typically, put the whole problem in sharp focus when he said, "We want a society that is sufficiently honest and open-minded to recognize its problems, sufficiently creative to conceive of new solutions, and sufficiently purposeful to put those solutions into effect . . . and we all know in our bones that what we do in education . . . has the greatest relevance to building the kind of society we want."

But what kind of educational system is that?

What is its relevance to democratic institutions, and to democracy in the broadest sense—as a process and a basic life style?

What is its relevance to the realities of our society— its strengths, its weaknesses, its grand purposes?

How does—and should—our educational system transmit our political heritage to each new generation?

How can it serve as a transmission belt and yet avoid imposing an oppressive strait jacket of conformity and an enforced orthodoxy?

Threading in and out of these questions' of "relevance" are still others: What democratic process, what democratic system of government, what democratic heritage are we really talking about? The one in our civics books? The one in the streets of our blighted cities? The one down at city hall? How about the process reflected in the way our schools and colleges actually operate?

These are the questions that define for us the tasks— the most fundamental tasks—with which we charge our educational system. In discussing them, I think we will shed some light on the directions in which our educational system ought to be tending.

First, a warning. We should not expect this educational system to resolve for itself those burning and unresolved political issues that range at large in our society. We should not expect our educational institutions to be free from conflict and tension among competing values when our society as a whole is fraught with these very tensions.

It is not free, and never should be, of the differences that mark a healthy society and define a democratic one.

We live in an intensely political society. We live politically in a society organized as a democratic republic. And this means, by its very definition, that your values are not necessarily mine, that our priorities may differ, and that not all our institutions can or should operate in the same fashion.

But, although our educational institutions exist in a political context, their business is not politics *per se.* Their business is not governing. Rather, their business is to discover, learn, and disseminate, to provide the benchmarks for the best path to the truth. Their authority is not based on a majority vote but on the disciplined pursuit of hard knowledge.

It is essential that we maintain this integrity and autonomy in the educational community. The freedom to think what one wants, to exchange ideas, to dissent —these are key ingredients in the intellectual process that the schools are in business to instill in the young. We do ourselves and our children a great disservice if we assume that all questions are foreclosed and that no generation can pose them anew.

Our young challenge us because of the differences, both seeming and real, between what we preach and what we do. And this is the issue, I think, that stands behind the so-called generation gap and every set of fresh demands—be they negotiable or nonnegotiable.

The issue, to put it most bluntly, is the hypocrisy that seems to pervade the society the young are about to inherit. It is the gulf between the ideal and the real, between an agenda of unsolved problems and the images of society mirrored by the media, by textbooks, and by parents and teachers.

In part, this hypocrisy sensed by the young can be attributed to youthful idealism. In part, also, it is a consequence of the gulf between the reality they sense and their present capabilities for coming to grips with it.

But society's institutions—and not least its educational institutions—must also share the blame. They
have fostered suspicions of hypocrisy in the young by
responding feebly to the demands for change. Many
institutions have not addressed themselves to the
urgency of the demands. Neither have they cultivated
the skills and techniques that those who are committed
to change must possess in order to move toward their
legitimate goals.

All too often we are stuffing the heads of the young
with the products of earlier innovation rather than
teaching them how to innovate. We treat their minds
as storehouses to be filled rather than as instruments
to be used.

We all subscribe, and genuinely, to the necessity of
teaching the process of critical inquiry. We do want
our youth to be free, but engaged, spirits.

But it is often quite a different story if Junior comes
home from school to report that his social studies class
has decided that the mayor—or maybe even a Cabinet
officer—is a scoundrel, has not been doing his job, and
ought unceremoniously to be dumped into the ashcan
of history.

And Junior and the community might also be
troubled, although perhaps in very different ways, if
a book by a leading American author is kept under
lock and key in the school library, although it is quite
visibly available in paperback at the corner drugstore.

Junior, his community, and his parents also might be
at odds over those things that "decent people just don't
talk about"—especially when these are the things that
Junior's peer group does almost nothing but talk about,

sometimes with blissful ignorance of fact and sometimes with appalling sophistication.

The way our schools and colleges treat their students and teachers tells its own lesson. And it may bear little resemblance to seminars on how democratic our way of life really is. This "performance gap" strikes at our vitals because it distorts idealism into cynicism and alienates our intellectuals.

It is understandable that the issues of our time inspire passion in debate, and this passion is healthy for a younger generation once feared to be apathetic and uncommitted. Social criticism which challenges us to live up to our professed beliefs can be a call to national renewal, not a symptom of national decay.

Free men cannot extend automatic support to every act of government. Moreover, it is extremely difficult, in the abstract, to fix precise limits for permissible restraint on the expression of dissent from government policy. I think the polarity of this tension, the dialogue on obedience, was established by Thoreau and Stephen Decatur. Thoreau said: "A free man owes fidelity to moral principles, to higher law, to conscience. Therefore, he must, or should, refrain from obeying an unjust and an immoral law." Yet, the objection to this argument is that if every citizen can judge the laws for himself, we do not have rule by law. We have anarchy.

For Stephen Decatur, as for Thoreau, it was a very simple matter: "My country, may she always be right, but my country, right or wrong."

Many will remember Chesterton's rebuttal to Decatur: "Saying 'my country, right or wrong,' is like saying, my mother, drunk or sober."

The great majority of the American people today

seems to realize there is a flaw in each of these simple answers. There is a minority at each end of the spectrum that is content with doctrinal purity, but most of us move back and forth along this spectrum.

The crux of the problem is how much dissent from a policy can be expressed without its being, or judged to be, unpatriotic.

But I believe it is intellectually dishonest to argue, as *Time* magazine and others have done, that dissent is not responsible unless the dissenter can offer a better alternative. That is desirable, of course, but you cannot apply that limit to dissent. It is tantamount to asking a baseball fan not to criticize the performance of a shortstop unless he is better at fielding grounders. I recall George Bernard Shaw's comment that he did not have to be able to lay an egg to know a rotten one when he tasted it.

But, judging by the behavior of some students, they could care less about the tradition of dissent. In their rhetoric, ostensibly about educational reform, they more resemble the forces of unreason. They worship the process of revolt itself. They seek not resolution but turmoil, not communication but confrontation.

There is an increasing willingness to embrace the language and the tactics of violence, to say the end justifies the means. But is the end to test and modify the system or to destroy it? If the goal is to destroy, then we have something akin to moral cowardice and a failure of good will that finally consumes the dissenter in his own hatreds.

Unless we expose these misconceptions of the democratic process, which seem to characterize the perspective of some of our youth today, our nation faces even more widespread disorder. Members of the intellectual establishment must assume a great share of the responsibility for countering this increasing tendency toward rule by mob action—the world of the demagogues and the rabble rousers.

To those who say there is no time for fine distinctions and no place for rational discourse in the struggle for power, let me say this: only the time that is taken and the tolerance that is shown can determine whether the nation's future course will or will not be perverted by an age of repression and regression. Over and over in the history of nations, this has been the clear alternative to rational dialogue. I think we are on the edge of that abyss today.

There is no question in my mind that it is the duty of an educational system to instill in young people respect for certain basic political values. Living as we do in a constitutional republic, we are committed to a set of propositions about man's proper relationship to the state. Even a casual perusal of *The Federalist* shows us the sophistication and endless political wisdom of those who drafted the Constitution.

That document contains a profound blueprint for the organization of government and for the channeling of social change. It also contains a Bill of Rights that, while specifying procedures for a democratic government, also describes ultimate values. The right to speak, to worship, to be accorded due process—these are ends of the good society as well as means of government.

Yet any attempt to inculcate political values creates grave difficulties, because we are committed to a constitutional framework and to a government that is

ultimately open-ended in its value structure. Political
or religious orthodoxy ought to be a matter never of
enforced national policy but always of free individual
choice.

Freedom is not something spoonfed in a civics class.
It is a state of being, and it must be experienced as a
matter of daily affirmation.

A thin but profound line thus separates education
from propaganda and indoctrination. If we attempt to
force our national heritage into a strait jacket of ortho-
dox values—even if we had a consensus—we stifle the
best of our creative minds.

But any course we adopt has its dangers and its problems. How do we train students in the methods of
critical inquiry so vital for the solution of our urgent
problems and, at the same time, avoid the creation of
cynicism or alienation? And when we consider these
questions, we should not unconsciously fall into the
elitist trap of wanting to train only the leaders of the
future. The quality of life and the political vitality of a
democracy, in large part, depend on the political knowledge and sophistication of the mass of people who
never will be names in a history book but whose hopes
and aspirations ultimately govern the nation's destiny.

In what direction should our educational institutions
move to correct existing deficiencies in inculcating
these values and this spirit of critical inquiry in our
student generation?

I harbor no illusions that the process of formal education either can or should always be a showcase for
participatory democracy. That would ignore, for instance, the necessary concept in education that it usual-

ly is the function of the one who knows more—the teacher—to impart knowledge to the student.

But I think our educational institutions increasingly will be forced to abandon the comforts of *in loco parentis* and examine critically, as the students increasingly have, the distinction between those privileges which may be withheld and those which are the national birthright of students as citizens. We cannot afford the cynicism engendered by wide discontinuities between the social science classroom and the real world of the student's total educational experience. And that includes the institutional arrangements of our schools and colleges in which we expect the students to learn to be citizens.

These conclusions are buttressed by hard facts. Current studies, incomplete as they are, have looked into the process of the political socialization of our children, and the conclusions are disconcerting to say the least.

For example, these studies indicate that, at the high school level, the traditional formal programs in political education have little or no positive influence on political beliefs and behavior, in or out of school. Other studies have shown that, even at the college level, the pervasive climate of opinion has a greater influence on political behavior than does formal instruction.

We will fail, too, if we think that our formal educational system operates in a vacuum, apart from the social matrix. By the time our students first enter kindergarten they have absorbed inputs measured literally in the thousands of hours from television and other media.

This knowledge is, to be sure, unstructured. But it is there, and it vitally affects the sophistication of the child. Dick-and-Jane textbooks can't hold a candle to "Captain Kangaroo," let alone "The Mod Squad." Unless our educational institutions both come to grips with the impact of this media explosion and then accommodate themselves to its implications for the learning process, we can expect our formal courses on political education to be just as unreal and ineffective—and just as irrelevant, if you please—as they have been in the past.

On the other hand, I am apprehensive about some proposals for reform. In some models, the classroom, if not abolished altogether, becomes mostly a convenient place for strategy sessions in the battle for social change. What we must strive for also is to teach the analytical and critical skills, refine the ability to analyze, distinguish and compare, and cultivate the ability to marshal and present arguments that are logical and based on fact.

Maybe this is enough. To indoctrinate as indisputable the values or policies that are in conflict and, in a free society, ought to be open to dispute glosses over the conflicts that are part and parcel of our democracy.

Our educational system may be endangered if it is seen as the immutable source of our values and policies. It is enough, I am saying, if it is seen—and upgraded —as a training ground in the method and the process by which each new generation fleshes out these values with its own preferred public policies.

Let me conclude with some observations close to my own heart. I believe, echoing Aristotle, that the ultimate end of political science is not knowledge but action. By this I do not for one moment denigrate the integrity of intellectual scholarship for its own sake.

But I think it is important to note that in politics, as in journalism, to be half right *on time* may be more important than to obtain the whole truth *too late*. Political participation is itself a form of education—a continuing process and a very humbling one. One must master what is perhaps the most difficult of tasks: to make decisions at times before all the facts are in.

A political official has to act, and often he must act to protect lives and property, before he is quite sure of the terrain. In such circumstances, if he were to wait until all the facts are known—until the future is part of the past—he would lose his capacity to influence the course of events. But this is education—politics *as* education—in its highest form, and in its greatest role in our continuing social drama.

If our educational institutions can transmit some sense of the continuing nature of political education, both in what they teach and how they operate as institutions, then we will not have to ask in each generation whether our educational institutions are relevant to a democratic society.

Raising the Issues

Ramsey Clark

IT'S TIME FOR CHANGE; ARE SCHOOLS UP TO IT?

IN 1921, H. G. Wells said it seemed to him that civilization was in a race between education and catastrophe. Since then, others, like George Wald, have come to believe the young see the winner and it is not education. Youth fears it is a generation without a future.

The catastrophe which spawned this fear of a futureless generation grows out of the vastness, the rapidity, and the acceleration of change. Change is the fundamental fact of our time. And the techniques by which we deal with change will be the key to whether and how we come through the turbulent years ahead.

At the risk of oversimplification, there are two dynamics which contribute most to change. One is science and technology. The other is population increase.

When the Constitution was ratified, there were 3.5 million immigrants in this country, sprinkled very lightly over the Eastern seaboard. Two cities—Philadelphia and New York—had populations of more than

RAMSEY CLARK is former United States Attorney General.

20,000. And only 5 per cent of the population lived in places which had as many as 2,500 people.

In October, 1967, the census clock in the Department of Commerce registered 200 million. But it failed to count 6 or 8 million—twice our population when the Federal Government was formed. It missed them because it could not count them. Some might say because the individual did not count any more—a mere 6 or 8 million people.

If we have added a lot of people in this century, a two-and-a-half-fold rise in population, we will add more before it's over. But compared to other countries, our increase is slow. The birth rate in the Philippines is twice ours. Half of the Brazilians are under sixteen while half of our people are over twenty-six. Over-all, the world population may increase by 1 billion people in the next ten years. There may be 3 or 4 billion more people in thirty-one years, as many more as there are altogether now. The impact on the individual will be immeasurable.

Science and technology, the other dynamic, has wrought more change in the daily life of America in one generation than was experienced in all previous history. In 1900, the Wright brothers were still working on bicycles. In December, 1903, they sustained manned flight in heavier-than-air craft for sixty-eight seconds. Barely half a century later, Sputnik circled the globe.

Marconi had a couple of patents in 1900. The next year he transmitted radio waves from Cornwall to Newfoundland. Sixty-seven years later we had the capability of instant audio-visual communications from any place in the world. There were more television sets by 1969 than people in 1900, and many school children born with television sets in the room spent more hours watching television than sitting in a classroom.

Our senior scientists did not dream of nuclear energy as schoolboys. Yet, today we can release from the atom powers of total destruction and energies far exceeding those of all the mules and fossil fuels that this world could ever hold.

Less than a generation after man first attained the ability to master many of the forces of nature, the question became whether technology—through which he achieved that mastery—would in turn master him. Technology offered greater risks than did gentle nature and often seemed more to shape new perils than to relieve old ones.

Population increase and developments in science and technology, as the principal forces of change, create turbulence in America that manifests itself clearly in areas of injustice and inequality. Principal among these has been racism as the plight of minorities. As science and population have compounded pressures for change and awareness of inequality, institutions have continued the leisurely adaptations of the nineteenth century.

As an illustration, fifteen years ago the Supreme Court decreed that all children had the constitutional right to an education in a public institution that was not segregated by race. It declared segregated schools inherently unequal.

But how have institutions respected this constitutional right? Nine years after *Brown* vs. *Board of Education* was decided 1 per cent of the black students in the public schools of the 11 states which had been the Confederacy were in desegregated schools. All deliberate speed at that rate means nine centuries. With the Civil Rights Act of 1964 came the guidelines. They were controversial because they worked. Some said we were going too fast. Some were more sympathetic with deliberate efforts to deny basic constitutional rights than with the education of young Negroes. Today, children who were in the first grade when *Brown* was decided are juniors in college.

But blacks, by and large, started dropping out six or eight years ago. They know that even today only 1 in 5 of the black public school students in the South are in desegregated schools. Over the fifteen years fewer than 1 in 20 has ever attended a desegregated school.

What does that mean? Among other things it means that the 2 million Negroes who have left the South in the 1960s for Watts, Hough, Harlem, and Central City, U.S.A., carry an immense educational disadvantage. Seventy per cent of the blacks in Watts at the time of the 1965 riots were born in the South. The children came from rural schools in Mississippi or South Carolina or urban schools in Birmingham or Houston. And even in the inferior schools of South Central Los Angeles, the children dropped back one year, two years, many never really continuing their education.

How incredible that we would permit this at a time when education is so essential to the individual, when it is his best, almost his only, chance for fulfillment in this technologically advanced world.

What have we done for Central City itself? Not much. Take a map of any major city in the United States. Mark the areas where the death rate is 25 per cent higher than for the city as a whole; where infant mortality is 4 times greater; where mental retardation from all its causes—malnutrition, the swallowing of lead-based paint that flaked off old tenement walls, brain damage during delivery, or early environment—is many times more common than for the whole city.

We boast of a nationwide unemployment rate that is below 4 per cent. We shouldn't. It is too high. It is also misleading. It is one of those facts that is the enemy of truth. It doesn't tell enough. Another fact that is the enemy of truth is that 25 per cent of the teen-age boys and 33 per cent of the teen-age girls in this country who are black and out of school are unemployed. That is a national average. There are places in every major city where 50 per cent of the employables are unemployed and the other 50 per cent underemployed. Mark those places on your map.

Mark the places where the old buildings stand. Half the buildings in Harlem were built before 1900, yet half the buildings in the world have been built in the last thirty years. The wiring in those buildings is fifty years old. Rats have chewed the insulation. There is no fire escape. Fires are common there and death and damage from them frequent. The ugliness of the environment erodes the quality of life. Everything comes apart, including families. Eighty per cent of the infants, children, and young people under eighteen years of age residing in Watts lived with one or neither parent in 1965.

There are places in each city where people have no rights in the real sense. A right is not what someone gives you but what no one can take from you. There is an uneasy order in these places, but little law. If the

poor save up and buy a television, as they do, and if
when they get it home the tube does not work, and the
person who sold it to them knew it when he sold it,
what can they do? Sue? How? If they are lucky they
may find a Neighborhood Legal Services Office or legal
aid, but the chances are very slim. The people who live
there have no power.

Crime can be located on the urban map. There are
high-crime areas in every city—places where a small
fraction of the people live and most of the crime occurs.
If you were poor and black, Puerto Rican, or Mexican-
American living in the urban slums, your chances of
being a victim of violent crime in 1967 was estimated
in a comprehensive study of one city as 1 in 77. If
you were white and lived in the suburbs in an economic
status above middle class, your chance of being a victim
of violent crime was 1 in 10,000. Violent crime is usually reported in the suburbs. It is not usually reported
in the ghetto.

In places where 15 per cent of the people live, 75
per cent of the arrests occur. That does not reflect the
proportion of crime. Nor does it mean that all the arrests are related to crime. Often it reflects society's
way of maintaining order without law. The cost of
police per capita there is several times higher than for
the city as a whole. Police presence is much higher,
but a breakdown of police-community relations inhibits
effective enforcement and limits both the safety and
the liberty of those who live there.

Need I tell you about the schools there? They will be
the most crowded. Many teachers will seek to transfer
out. There will be some teachers seeking to transfer
to the ghetto to teach, but school administrators will

be very cautious about them. That may sound strange, but that is a fact. There will be fewer certified teachers there than in other schools and fewer teachers in proportion to the student body. The classrooms will be the most turbulent in the district, supplies the scarcest, books fewer and older. The dropout rate will be far higher than elsewhere, and the average dropout will be much younger than those in the rest of the city. The principals there are so concerned, and need be, about just maintaining order that order has become their main goal—merely to avoid a major disturbance. It is very like many of the youth detention centers, where the warden has one goal: to hold the place together, to prevent a riot, to get the troublemakers out as fast as possible before they cause trouble.

It was of such a ghetto school that the teacher in *Up the Down Staircase* despaired. How can those children be given a good education when they are in school six hours a day, five days a week, thirty-six weeks a year, and the rest of the time the ghetto is their classroom?

We cannot go on like this very much longer. Institutions must address themselves to the problems and needs of minorities. Our failure to end racism adds immensely to student unrest. Students see racism and rotting cities on television four hours a day and become impatient with Latin conjugation. When thousands are starving in Biafra, they are reading about the Franco-Prussian War for the third time. When Vietnam rages on, they are reading about the Constitutional Fathers. From mass communication, they see that much of what they learn in school is irrelevant.

If individuals do not learn to deal with the problems

of this world—to analyze them, to face them—when they are young, when can we expect that they might? If, when they are in their school years, they do not establish the traditions, attitudes, habits, a sense of what is right and what is wrong, of what is permissible and what is not permissible, of liberty and what is essential to its preservation, of humanity and individuality, will it ever happen? Their character is forming now. They will live with it for the rest of their lives.

Students are concerned with the problems—like racism and war—that are facing this country today. Yet they see themselves in a mass society—made less individualistic by population increase and technological developments—as unable to affect, in the least way, things vital and important to them. This includes their own education. They want to be involved. And we have to disenthrall ourselves and think anew and act anew and involve them.

We have to deal with the future, which is changing, changing in ways and at rates that we barely perceive. We must test every fact and principle with freedom, curiosity, and skepticism. We have to learn from relevant history how to instill in our young a sense of individual dignity, a reverence for life when you are conditioned by nearly everything in your life to violence. How do you instill a sense of the dignity of the individual when you have 3,000 kids in a high school and the only ones that are known are the football players, the troublemakers, and half a dozen others? Well, you can, and you can make schools relevant to the issues of the day, to the divisions of the day. If you do not, the great turbulence that we are caught in will increase and the opportunity that it provides will be lost.

It is change that causes revolution, and not revolution, change. It always has been that way. No people ever rose from dormancy and overcame.

Turbulence should not be shunned, even if it could be, because it is a life force. Shaw said of Beethoven that he was the most turbulent spirit that ever found expression in pure sound. Without turbulence, he would have been a second-rate composer. We can capture this turbulence, and we can employ it in our greatest industry: education. Education involves nearly a third of our people as student, teacher, or administrator. Education must be reshaped to meet the needs of the day.

And as we do this we must remember that while some crave order and others seek justice, the long history of man says, in school or in life, you will have neither order nor justice unless you have both.

Raising the Issues

Gerald W. Marker and Howard D. Mehlinger

SCHOOLS, POLITICS, REBELLION, AND OTHER YOUTHFUL INTERESTS

THE FACT that an increasing number of American high schools have experienced serious rebellion is not surprising. What is remarkable is that such rebellion has been so long in coming and so slow to adopt political forms. For, if it is true that college students rebel against meaningless courses and perceived restrictions on their freedom, then the high schools should have become centers of discontent long ago. Compared to high schools, colleges provide a wide range of courses from which students can choose. High school students are only now becoming fully conscious of the ways in which their lives are enclosed by a fence of rules, customs, and procedures imposed by adults intent upon shaping them to society. As their consciousness grows, high school rebellions can be expected to escalate.

If we think about schools in the customary way, rebellious youth can be explained only by customary

GERALD W. MARKER is Coordinator of Social Studies, Indiana University, and HOWARD D. MEHLINGER is Director, High School Curriculum Center in Government, Indiana University.

terms: juvenile delinquent, hoodlum, vandal. But studies of today's rebellious youth suggest that these terms are not appropriate. To account for the thoughtful, serious youth who have emerged as leaders of the new rebellion, we must search for new perspectives, the perspectives, perhaps, of those who are rebelling.

The high school is an institution established by society to prepare children for adult status. High school is expected to transmit the values, knowledge, and skills that children will require if they are to play adult roles successfully.

Consequently, adults decide what will be taught, who will teach, how the school will operate, and what resources should be allocated for education. Professionals are recruited to conduct the school's business. These professionals, presumably expert in the knowledge to be transmitted and in how children learn, include both teachers and administrators. While the school is established to serve the needs of its student-clients, the school is also an arm of the government, responsible to a public constituency. This means that both teachers and administrators must somehow balance the demands made upon the system by students against the claims of parents and taxpayers.

Teachers and administrators are recruited, serve voluntarily, and are paid for their services. Students are assigned to schools, are required to attend by law, and receive only symbolic rewards. Students have little control over how they will spend their six- to seven-hour day, little choice over who will teach them, or what they will study. While students are at school, they become subject to the authority of school officials.

The school system is responsible for a product that meets at least minimum levels of quality: all children must be able to read, to write, to count. But the product is by no means uniform; some children achieve a level of competence beyond that of their peers. School administrators must move many students through the school system, making certain that each child has an opportunity to learn what is expected but also making certain that students do not dally at any one grade level. This would overload and unbalance the system. As students move through the system by age grades, they are taught what has been decided by adults is appropriate for students to learn. High school teachers are differentiated according to subject specialities.

The school administrator worries about the general efficiency of the system. He must make certain that a sufficient number of staff members have been recruited to perform each of the assigned tasks. He must build and maintain buildings near where students live. He must see that students are fed, kept warm and comfortable, and transported to and from school. He must be concerned that the end product of the twelve-year sequence resembles what the community wants. Rarely do administrators, especially superintendents, have continuous and direct contact with the student-clients.

The details for carrying out the primary task of the schools—instruction—is left to the teacher. In this role, he may expect a number of conflicts. First of all, he is likely to face students who have no special desire to learn what he wishes to teach. They did not choose his course but were assigned to him by a counselor, a member of the administrative team. While a teacher has some flexibility regarding how the course will be

taught, he is expected to cover specified content during
the year in order that his students will be ready for the
courses that lie ahead. Even the books he will use often
have been chosen by others, perhaps a state textbook
committee, an administrator, sometimes a committee
of teachers.

When the teacher meets his students, new conflicts
arise. The learning process is a highly affective experience, occurring most profitably when there is mutual
trust and confidence between teacher and student. Yet,
in nearly every high school classroom across the nation, teachers seeking to establish a proper classroom
climate for learning struggle to impose their authority
over the class, thereby reducing their chances to establish optimum learning conditions. This is not a criticism
of the teacher who does this; rather it is a charge
against the entire system that makes such a practice
necessary. Only the most charismatic, brilliant, or fool-
hardy teacher would act differently, because the
chances for disaster are great. Students are quick to
seize the initiative and win the battle before the teacher
can mount a counterattack. Moreover, while school
systems want teachers who can teach, even more they
want teachers who can maintain order. The quickest
way to be criticized by colleagues and administrators
is to lose control of the class.

But the conflict between the staff and the students
is not primarily a contest of strength. Schools have
invented a system of rules and bribes to maintain control. Students are regimented through a school day with
little or no free time of their own. At many schools,
the outer doors are not unlocked until a few minutes
before school begins each morning; they are locked

again shortly after school closes in the afternoon and students have left the building. Once admitted to the building, students are kept under close surveillance. They are carefully programmed from one classroom to another. Throughout the day students move from one class to another according to a schedule planned by the administration. Little time is allowed for passing between classes. During such times teachers are stationed in the hallways to make certain the flow of students is continuous. A bell rings, signaling the start of a new period, and each student must be in his seat. Late arrivals are sent to the office to secure written permission to enter or are punished by being forced to remain late after school.

Throughout the day, the movement of students is carefully controlled. If a student leaves a class, he must have the permission of his teacher and a signed pass that provides details about where he originates, where he is going, what time he left, and the reason for his trip—even if it is to the drinking fountain. A student apprehended without a pass is treated much as a citizen in an alien country without a passport. To check on passes, to prevent vandalism, and to enforce school rules, some schools have established squads of senior boys and girls to act as agents for the administration. In return for special privileges they sit at the ends of corridors acting as checkpoints, or they roam the corridors, restrooms, and parking lots searching for student offenders.

Violations of rules can result in various forms of punishment: a lecture by a teacher or an administrator, forced confinement of from fifteen minutes to an hour after school, a deprivation of something a student values such as his right to drive a car to school, or paddling. Those who believe corporal punishment is declining in our society have not visited the schools. In one large urban high school, paddlings are administered publicly in the hallway as a lesson to other students.

But, it is not the system of punishment that is the principal mechanism of control in the school. One of the bribes is the program of extracurricular activities, planned and carefully supervised by adults. As will be shown later, student values toward school are oriented much more to the extracurricular activities of the school than they are to the school's central purpose. The school subtly uses the extracurricular activities as a device to control the student body.

For example, athletics may serve as a harmless outlet for expressing hostility against the school. Athletes must meet certain grade and attendance requirements in order to be eligible to play football and other sports; in some schools the faculty has a major hand even in the selection of cheerleaders. The student government is encouraged to develop codes on student conduct, dress, and hair style. Administrators know that codes facilitate control, and it is easier to legitimize the punishment of students if the code has been written by students.

The choice laid before a student government is rarely whether a code is necessary. The choice is usually whether the students will write the code or whether the faculty will write it.

The evaluation of student performance is another control device. In addition to objective measurements, students are evaluated according to such criteria as participation in class discussion, attitudes toward work, and citizenship. In short, nearly all teachers manipulate grades to some degree or another to accommodate these subjective elements. In this way there is subtle but powerful pressure on students to behave in a manner acceptable to teachers.

The typical high school employs people who listen to but do not act upon the grievances of students. There is no ombudsman to intervene on behalf of the students with the bureaucracy. Counselors are really tools for administrators, despite the professional ideology of counseling. Who can a student complain to if his teacher is incompetent, is lazy, is a racist? A student must either accommodate himself to the situation or rebel—silently, by dropping out of school or by turning in poor work or overtly, by setting fire to trash cans and triggering fire alarms.

Due process is not available to students. When students are accused by teachers of violations of school rules, they already stand convicted. There is no presumption of innocence until evidence is heard. No witnesses are called; no opportunity is afforded the student to defend himself. The administration and the teaching faculty of a school form a united front to maintain control, and a principal, even when he suspects the teacher is wrong, is more likely to take the side of the teacher than that of the student. He feels obliged to maintain teacher morale.

In short, the official structure of the school is primarily an authoritarian bureaucracy that shapes students according to adult expectations. Most students learn to cope with the school system. But while they do so, they may not be learning practices that are consistent with democratic principles and ideals.

It should be recognized that teen-agers are a remarkable subgroup in American society, perhaps unique in human history. It is a group with its own symbols, language, values, status system, interests, and activities. A flow of children moves through this adolescent society before they emerge to accept roles as adult citizens. The culture of American teen-agers is not only influenced by the total American society, but it in turn influences the total society.

American teen-agers are unique in other ways. As a group they are remarkably affluent and incredibly sophisticated. They know far more, are more worldly-wise, than their parents or grandparents at the same age. Yet, as a group, they have no responsibility for the major decisions that affect them. They are subject to the demands of adults. They are people who are being prepared to be something other than they are now. Many adolescents believe they are being molded without their control for roles in life that they do not want. Adults believe they do these things for the teen-agers' own good.

Many students, of course, are quite capable of accommodating themselves to the authority structure and the values of the school. Some do not; from this group come the instigators of rebellion. At first glance they seem to be the problem, but a more serious problem may actually exist with those who have accommodated.

Those who have studied the American high school have given us a vivid description of its peer culture. While there are differences among schools, it is clear that the things students value are not the same things officially sanctioned by the schools. For example, a decade ago Coleman found that the most admired boys tended to be the best athletes and the most popular with girls, rather than the best students. The most admired girls tended to be those most active in extra-curricular activities and those most sought after for dates, rather than the best students. Nevertheless, Coleman found there were some differences among the high schools he studied regarding the bases of status in the peer culture. We believe additional factors have appeared since his study. There seem to be regional differences in adolescent peer culture. Politicization of the peer culture seems to be more advanced ` in the far western and eastern high schools than it is in midwestern and southern high schools. Moreover, changes seem to have occurred within schools.

Today, black youths frequently acquire status as leaders of black militant causes, and many intellectual white boys clearly are admired by girls who share their political beliefs. It appears also that the role of girls in the peer culture of some high schools is changing. No longer are some girls content to stand on the sidelines and cheer for male athletes. Increasingly, they have become coleaders of political movements, along with boys. Whether the leading group of a given high school gains status through athletics, dating, automobiles, or political activity, the fact remains that the sources of prestige among adolescents bear little relationship to the official norms and values of the school. The teacher's pet rarely is the most influential among his peers.

What occurs in a typical classroom is similar to what

occurs on a prison farm or on the assembly line of a factory. Just as prisoners sent out to mow roadside ditches frequently do as little as possible and industrial workers sometimes use group pressure to make certain that ambitious workers do not exceed quotas, so students struggle with teachers to secure a reduced work load. Sometimes the conspiracy is raised to the conscious level and is planned; more often it is unspoken but understood. Most experienced teachers silently participate in the conspiracy by adjusting the work load according to the kinds of students enrolled in the course. Students have a significant influence on the teacher's expectations for the class. Students who do extra work or perform brilliantly on lessons are threats to the work norms of the group and are subject to pressure. As teachers cannot fail all the students, they strive to find a point where most students can pass and in the process lower their standards.

Therefore, while the initial reaction may lead one to believe that school might be an intolerable place for a free spirit, in fact students are able to blunt the school's drive sufficiently to make it a reasonably happy place to be, especially if one is a member of the leading clique in school. In exchange for accommodating oneself to the school ritual and accepting school authority without complaint, an adolescent is free to pursue the extracurricular activities through which he wins the prestige and status of his peers. The school on the other hand gains order and a successful extracurricular program.

About the only way a school administrator can clash seriously with the leading clique of students is by interfering directly in the things they value most, their source of status and prestige. For example, teachers find it easier to control their classes if they accept the status system created by the students. If they try to tamper with this, by imposing new leaders or by failing to defer to student leaders, they encounter difficulty. When one considers how important personal appearance is to adolescents, it is apparent that a principal who tries to impose his notions about hair style and dress length on the leading group is merely asking for trouble.

But, what of those students who like others find the school goals unattractive and who also are unsuccessful in extracurricular activities and in gaining membership in the leading cliques of the school? In other words, what is the status of lower-class adolescents who make poor grades, do not participate in extracurricular activities, and are socially inept? It was this group that spawned most of yesterday's rebels. What has been their status in school?

At the present time, the high school serves as a device to keep many young men and women off the job market. Presumably, the high school will prepare them for jobs for which they are ineligible without a high school diploma. By compulsory attendance laws or by parental pressure, many students remain in high school today who in earlier times would have quit school.

It has been shown that most rebellious high school youth are found in this group. These students feel no strong attachment to the school's goals. They do not find the curriculum of the school meaningful for the kinds of jobs they know they will fill. Moreover, ostracized by the leading peer groups, they tend to identify more with adult models. These students tend to be contemptuous of leading peer groups and demand to be treated as adults. Teachers and administrators, unable to accept them as adults, find them to be a constant source of tension.

Whatever irritations these students have caused school officials, they could always be explained away. They were labeled juvenile delinquents, troublemakers, vandals, etc. *They* were the problem, not the system. In fact, the aid of socially prominent students has often been enlisted against these students. But, school officials cannot so easily explain away the new, highly politicized form of rebellion that is occurring in the schools today.

What seems to be different about the newest rebellion is both its style and its source. Earlier rebellions were by students who were alienated both from the school and from the peer culture. They were less sophisticated and more likely to become apathetic, nonparticipating adult citizens. The leaders of the current high school rebellion are those who are members of leading groups in the school. Becoming conscious of what the school has become and the general failure of the present system, they are seeking to change it.

The rebellion in the high school is no longer limited to random acts of vandalism but assumes the shape of sophisticated political tactics. The rebellious youth are no longer the lonely and the alienated but the school intellectuals. The irony of the present situation is that school officials are often in the position of having to punish the brightest and most committed students in the school, the very type of student the school ought to be most proud to have educated.

One task schools accept as legitimate is to prepare

students for the role of citizen. To satisfy this goal, schools have established courses that provide students with the knowledge and attitudes they will require to be useful citizens and some extracurricular activities that afford students the opportunity to practice the skills of democratic participation. Practice in the skills of democratic participation means primarily practice in oral discussion, parliamentary procedure, and voting. As a rule, student governments are not permitted to deal with issues that cut deeply through the school: how to balance the desire to smoke on the part of some students with the demands of the school board and administration that smoking not be permitted on school property. Rather, student governments tend to cope with issues about which there is relatively little controversy. Most student governments operate in a very circumscribed environment, and even then their decisions are subject to administrative veto.

American history is most often taught as a chronological survey of the history of the United States from the period of the early Western European explorers to the present day. The focus is on elections, wars, treaties, and boundary disputes. Students read about the efforts of courageous white men and women who built a strong, powerful nation despite an initially hostile environment. The contributions of minority groups are diminished. American culture heroes—George Washington, Thomas Jefferson, Benjamin Franklin—are treated at length; controversies that cut and tore into American society are mentioned—but muted.

Civics and government courses are primarily a combination of legalistic descriptions and ethical prescriptions. The focus is upon government and a formal description of its agencies and operations. Citizens are described as people who have an obligation to obey the law and to vote, an act that affords each individual an equal chance to influence the government. Generally ignored are the realities of the political process itself.

While the authors know many social studies teachers who are exceptions to the rule and who conduct lively classes that deal intellectually and responsibly with central issues in American society, in general, social studies classes are more like catechism classes than the inquiry-oriented centers of freewheeling discussion they are claimed to be. Teachers conduct recitations over the facts covered by the reading assignment or lead discussions on such questions as, "Should a Congressman vote as his conscience dictates or as his constituents expect him to vote?"

From the latter part of the question, teachers tend to move in one of two directions, either letting each student state his opinion—perhaps even calling for a show of hands to see which opinion is most widely held in class—or supporting some students' comments and downgrading others, thereby confirming in the students' minds the opinion they are to hold. In the first instance, opinions are treated like votes, to be counted and weighed equally, with the result that students feel no need to examine the bases for their beliefs. In the second instance, the teachers assert that they want students to express their views freely, but the message that gets through is that the teacher truly wants only those views that conform to his. A variety of studies have shown teachers to be generally passive, concerned about their own security, conservative in outlook, and dogmatic in attitudes. From such teachers one should expect little more than confirmation of adult and community norms.

Civics and government classes tend to be places where teachers talk a great deal and students play it safe. Facts, not inquiry, rule. The instruction is relatively harmless, unless you believe that it is harmful to deprive students of the realities of the political process. Certainly, no businessman would look to the civics course in his high school for advice on how to cope with the political structure of his community.

In the 1950s, adolescents were accused of being too apathetic or not caring enough about important social and political issues. No such charges are leveled against the youth of the late 1960s. What has happened?

We believe students are attempting to reduce the inconsistencies they perceive between what they are taught about the American political system and the realities of the school environment within which they live. Students participate directly in two political worlds: the authority structure of the school and the authority structure of their own peer culture. Some students are participating directly in a third political world: local and national politics. From his civics teacher a student learns about an American political system in which all men are born with inalienable rights; yet some of these rights and privileges are unavailable to him at school. He learns that every man has an equal opportunity to become President; yet in his own peer group he knows that he faces handicaps that prevent him from becoming a school leader. (Or if he is a leader, he did not become so by the routes described in the Constitution.) As a participant in civil-rights causes and the Vietnam War debate, he has

gained firsthand knowledge of citizen participation. He
has learned that the ideal world described in the civics
and government classes does not always conform to
the real world he is experiencing directly. In the 1950s
many students reacted to these inconsistencies by
dropping out, psychologically.

Today, the inconsistencies remain, but some students have decided that it is not necessary to drop out.
It is possible to try to reform the real institutions within which one lives to try to bring them into line with
democratic ideals. Such students demonstrate their
commitment to the free, open, democratic society they
have been taught to value. Today they are demanding
that the school live up to society's own values. For the
most part, the civics and government courses with
their emphasis upon voting as *the* participatory act
remain as unrealistic as they were in the past. What
has occurred recently is that students have acquired
new models of political activity. Some of these models
stem from civil-rights leaders of the late 1950s and
early 1960s; other models are student protest leaders
in colleges and universities. An increasing number are
high school students.

Students have learned that voting is not the only
participatory act possible. One can sit in, march, speak,
petition, and confront. It is possible to overload even
the most authoritarian structure until it listens and
begins to pay attention to what the clients are demanding. If the administration will not permit free discussion in the school newspaper, one can print his own
newspaper and distribute it to students. If student leaders are merely puppets of the administration, it is possible to organize and choose student leaders who are

more responsive to student demands. If an administration will not listen, it is even possible to close down the institution.

The irony is that the schools have long urged students to be concerned with social issues and accept the value that they should participate. Now students want to participate, to help make the rules under which they live, and the schools are unprepared to cope with the political energy of their clients.

What type of response should we expect schools to make to this challenge? If the school is truly an authoritarian, bureaucratic system, as we have described, we should expect that its initial response will be that of all authoritarian, bureaucratic systems that are under attack: it will tighten controls and increase pressure for conformity. Therefore, we may expect restrictions on extracurricular activities (deprive students of rewards), an increase in the number of police in school (increase surveillance and control), and growth in the number of expulsions. Such is the behavior expected of authoritarian, bureaucratic regimes the world over.

On the other hand, the school might undertake a critical self-study to learn if it is truly accomplishing its purposes and is fully meeting the needs of its clients. It could turn to its student-clients and to the community it serves for advice, rather than acting defensively. This would be the kind of response we tell students they should expect from free, democratic institutions that have been created to serve their constituents.

Raising the Issues

The Conference Film

"SHORT TAKES FROM A BAD SCENE"

Conference participants were shown a film consisting of excerpts from several motion pictures. It was not intended to be an objective, balanced report. Said the film's producers: "The questions we have tried to raise and the points of view expressed mainly reflect the interests of the students themselves."

The film was shot primarily in predominantly white, middle-class urban and suburban areas.

> (*Scene I—a meeting of the board of education in a very wealthy suburban district. Representatives of a new, militant student organization are appearing before the board.*)

STUDENT A: It is really sort of contradictory. Students [are] asked when they are out of school to vote, asked

THE CONFERENCE FILM was assembled by Guggenheim Productions, Inc. (*Scenes I* and *IX*), with excerpts from several films including: "What They Want To Produce, Not What We Want To Become" (*Scenes II, III, V, VI, VII,* and *VIII*), a part of Canadian Broadcasting Corporation's *Public Eye* series, copyright Canadian Broadcasting Corporation; and Frederick Wiseman's "High School" (*Scene IV*), copyright © 1968, Organization for Social and Technical Innovation.

to take part in our democracy, and yet in school they are told, "Well, you're not citizens, you're students."

STUDENT B: The student doesn't have the right to analyze the school, to criticize the school beyond a few very limited areas. If he does, then he's told by all the human beings in the system he's doing something very wrong.

STUDENT A: The way the question was phrased was, "What kind of students do we want to turn out?" Well, what we are suggesting is that we've got to stop turning out students and viewing them as a product. And so, you know, one day you might set up an educational system where you have people exploring different ideas, and you might not know what you're going to turn out.

STUDENT C: Learning has become a task. It's become a job just like people's jobs have become when they become bored with them. And I think students are becoming bored with tasks that have merely been placed on them as a burden. I think that what has happened, you see, is that the student will go to school and his learning is done in the school, and outside of the school his living is done. And learning and living have become two separate entities. One of the things we have to strive for is to bridge that gap and make learning a real living experience and to make it a worthwhile experience, to make it an enjoyable experience, which learning can be.

STUDENT A: When a student . . . enters school in the elementary grades, the child has a natural curiosity, he has a desire to learn. He wants to go to school because it is a place of stimulating ideas—new ways of expressing himself. But by the time that student has finally reached high school, somewhere in that time this desire to learn, this desire to come to school for an education, has been completely lost.

STUDENT B: What do you plan to do? How do you plan on acting on these statements? How soon can some of these things start to be carried out? You are elected officials. Therefore, you are responsible to your constituents, who don't happen to be the students. Although we're the ones in school, it is our parents who, more or less, control you, and if we express the need for something, say, a majority of the people who have voted you in office don't want, then you try to carry it out and you might not get voted back in office. So, you know, we have some really hard things we are really going to have to get around, and I think we are going to have to start talking how we are going to get started enacting some of these proposals.

SCHOOL BOARD MEMBER: We have given the authority and the responsibility to the professional staff to operate a school system. All of our citizenry who pay taxes in the county are footing the bill for this. They have to be convinced they are getting their money's worth or we'll not continue to get the support. Now these are kind of the realities of life, and we're talking about matters of degree. That's the essence of it as I see it. There is room for improvement, but, in my opinion, I think the school system does very well. It must not do too bad or you wouldn't all be here today.

STUDENT B: Could I just make a brief comment? So far as that is concerned, we're here in spite of the school system and not [because of] it.

(Scene II—an interview with a high school principal.)

PRINCIPAL: The public may think the schools are democratic. They are democratic as far as the rights of the individual, but as far as the operation, they are not democratic. In order to get efficiency in a school system, there has to be a clear pattern of operation, behavior, rules, and regulation. Then there's not time for a group of people to sit down and thrash out a variety of ideas and to come up with a quick, clearcut, and efficient policy. There has to be one individual who has been selected because of his training, because of his experience, because of his drive and know-how that is put in charge. And within reason, then, his philosophy would be interpreted into a policy which would be the policy of operation of that school. Now I believe that's basic—how you get an efficient school.

It is not the desire of the principal to have an atmosphere of fear, but yet there has to be someone strong. There has to be what you might call a figurehead that stands for something, that will impress upon everyone that if we do not follow regulations, there can be punishment. Now to that extent, of course, there could be said to be some fear in the operation of a well-disciplined school.

(Scene III—an interview with a female teacher.)

INTERVIEWER: What kind of respect does a school system give to children?

TEACHER: Well, in my experience it's very limited. We can go through their desks, we can look in their lockers, we can take notes that they're passing. We can bring them down and put them in a situation where they have to betray a confidence to a friend, where they have to squeal on other kids. They have really no privacy at all. We can pry into every aspect of their lives.

INTERVIEWER: But guidance counselors and others would say that this is done out of a concern to help them. What do you think about that?

TEACHER: I think in many cases it probably is.

INTERVIEWER: And what's the result? Can you help kids this way? What kind of environmental situation do you create in fact?

TEACHER: Well, you don't help a child by telling him you respect him and his rights as an individual and his integrity as an individual and then force him to put up his hand to ask if he can go to the bathroom or to go out the door to get a drink, or send him home because he's forgotten his books, or send him to the office because he doesn't want to work. You don't force a child to learn self-control by regimenting every moment, so that he doesn't ever have to make a decision.

(*Scene IV—the office of a physical education teacher.*)

TEACHER: What do you mean you can't take gym? Do you get dressed in the morning?

BOY: Yes.

TEACHER: Do you get undressed?

BOY: Yes.

TEACHER: Well, you can get into a gym outfit.

BOY: Yeah, I know.

TEACHER: All right, you get into a gym outfit.

BOY: I am going to the doctor today.

TEACHER: Now, look, you'd better be in a gym outfit. We'll determine whether you take exercise or not. We'll determine that.

BOY: I am not going to argue with you, but I am not going to take gym. I am not even supposed to come to school.

TEACHER: I'm going to tell you something. Don't you talk, you just listen. You come prepared in a gym outfit when you go to gym, is that clear? All right. Now we are going to put you in an uncompromising position, but you'll come dressed in a gym outfit.

(*Scene V—the interview with the school principal continues.*)

INTERVIEWER: Do you think that the way you run your school is unusual in this country or is it fairly typical?

PRINCIPAL: No, I would be inclined to think that probably I am a little tougher. I run a little closer, tighter organization. But it is the only kind of organization I know. It is the only kind I have ever run. My teachers stay with me and like the protection I give them, and I do protect my teachers. The young people adjust to it, 98 per cent of them. We turn out a product. We pass examinations. We get jobs in industry—commercial and technical. You can't beat success.

(*Scene VI—an interview with a student.*)

INTERVIEWER: How do teachers let you know what kind of person they want you to be? You've got to

figure it out. How do you know it, how did you
learn it?

STUDENT: Well, I guess I learned it a long time ago
when they teach you to sit still, and keep quiet, and
not put your hand up too often, not talk, don't chew
gum, things like that. That is how you learn it.

INTERVIEWER: How do they teach it? What power do
they use to get you to do that? To sit still, to not
talk.

STUDENT: Well, whatever they need, they have.

(*Scene VII—interview with woman teacher continues.*)

WOMAN TEACHER: What difference does it make if kids
are talking in the hall? What difference does it make
if they are walking two or three abreast? What difference does it make if they are chatting to their
friends when they come in the room or when they
are walking to the next classroom? People say we
are training them for later life so they'll know how
to control themselves. Where do you ever see adults
walking in single file, never talking to the person in
front of them, or the person behind? Most of the
time they are simply meeting frustration, they are
trying to judge what you want, what you want to
hear, what is the right thing to say, what is going
to make an impression on you, how they are going to
get through grade eight.

INTERVIEWER: Is that what you personally want them
to do?

WOMAN TEACHER: No, I'd like them to try and figure
out who they are and who the other people in the

room are and who I am. To find some excitement in learning, find excitement in getting to know other people.

INTERVIEWER: Well, if you the teacher want that, why doesn't it happen in your classroom?

WOMAN TEACHER: Well, occasionally it does, but we don't have time. We are pressed to cover specific amounts of material which have to be tested to get them through this chunk of their education to move on to the next chunk.

Some children learn a great deal and these are the ones who get through our systems. They know what we want. They memorize the text. A child said to me the other day, "It is no problem to pass exams, I can memorize, but two days later I haven't the faintest idea what I learned. It doesn't have any meaning for me." And this is the problem. The learning is not integrated. What they learn does not become a part of them. It is something to be spewed back on examination.

(*Scene VIII—an interview with a high school student.*)

INTERVIEWER: Mary, how long have you known how to play the system in school?

STUDENT: I think I've known since about grade four.

INTERVIEWER: Grade four? How did you learn way back then?

STUDENT: Well, I [had] just read a book on the solar system and the teacher had taught us on the solar system and this came up on the exam. I put down what the teacher had told us rather than what I thought, because this would get me the marks.

INTERVIEWER: Did it?

STUDENT: Uh-huh. I got the highest mark.

INTERVIEWER: So you've gone from grade four all the way through elementary school and high school knowing this.

STUDENT: Uh-huh.

INTERVIEWER: Has it succeeded?

STUDENT: Oh, I think so.

INTERVIEWER: Do you think most of the students who get high marks in school get them the same way you do?

STUDENT: I think so, because I know the girl who gets the highest mark in English has the formulas down even more than I do. She knows exactly what to put, and her writing sounds kind of childish, but it is the formula and it gets the marks.

INTERVIEWER: What do you think about adults who you can handle as easily as this?

STUDENT: Well . . . you don't have any feeling for them, really. You just feel that it is kind of a business arrangement. You give them the paper, they give you the marks.

(Scene IX—a voice speaks.)

NARRATOR: The students are told, they say, that good grades are the key to success in school and therefore in life. They are pressed to finish college and then to slip quietly into the good life with all the rewards of success, but even here, in this cushioned and carefully arranged world, they can't be shut off from the sights and sounds of that large and real world beyond —a world that appears to bear less and less relationship to all this neatness and order.

Today more and more young people speak of an adult world deaf to injustice, blind to hypocrisy, a world they see as increasingly smug and self-centered, and they are speaking out against it more loudly every day.

Historically, injustice is not new, nor is hypocrisy. Neither is student unrest, nor an establishment bent on maintaining order by force, if necessary. What is entirely new is the way young people have learned to look at life and to perceive at once its glaring inconsistencies. From birth they have been immersed in TV and they see the world through the eyes of its prophet, Marshall McLuhan.

The electronic environment makes an information level outside the schoolroom that is far higher than the information level inside the schoolroom. In the nineteenth century, the knowledge inside the schoolroom was higher than the knowledge outside. Today it is reversed. The child knows that in going to school he is, in a sense, interrupting his education.

One of the Montgomery County students summed it up this way, "I think what has happened," he said, "is that a student's learning is supposed to be done in a school and his living done outside the school. Learning and living have become two separate entities." And what we have to strive for is to make learning a real living experience, a worthwhile and exciting experience.

Facing the Issues

Alan F. Westin

RESPONDING TO REBELS WITH A CAUSE

MY CENTER, the Center for Research and Education in American Liberties of Columbia University and Teachers College, attempting to evolve new models of civic education for the 1970s, has been examining the implications of the militant movement among secondary-school students. Preliminary results of our survey are cause for serious concern.

Since November, 1968, the center has subscribed to a press-clipping service that covers 1,800 daily newspapers in the country. We instructed the clipping service to send us only accounts of serious disruptions in the schools: strikes, sit-ins, boycotts, protest demonstrations, and riots.

During November, December, January, and February, there were 239 serious disruptions involving 348 high schools in 38 states and the District of Columbia. The number of clippings this spring has increased

ALAN F. WESTIN, Director of the Center for Research and Education in American Liberties, is Professor of Public Law and Government at Columbia University.

almost threefold, indicating a sharp rise in the rate of high school conflict.

Though many of these disruptions involved several types of issues simultaneously, we found that the incidents could be separated into five main classes: racial (132 schools in 27 states); political (81 schools in 21 states); dress codes (71 schools in 25 states); educational reform issues (17 schools in 14 states); and school discipline (60 schools in 28 states).

What is particularly significant is that these disruptions have taken place in every part of the country, in every type of school and every type of community. From our survey, we have no difficulty in accepting the results of a random sample that secondary-school principals conducted at their annual convention last month, in which 60 per cent of the sample reported significant "student protests" in their high schools.

I am sure that there are quite diverse viewpoints as to the causes and implications of such high school protests. There are some who will see this as another legacy of social permissiveness and the breakdown of family, legal, and moral standards in contemporary America. There will be strong assumptions that the issues are more manufactured than real, that S.D.S. organizers and black militants are creating such incidents as part of an organized campaign to disrupt the schools. There are some who probably see this as a long-delayed and welcome revolt by youth against an authoritarian school bureaucracy, an irrelevant and boring secondary-school curriculum, and the racist policies and attitudes that most black students encounter in their schools. There may even be some who will see this as the convulsive eruptions of the new electronic generation intent on dissolving outmoded, pre-electronic institutional forms and creating a more direct-experience oriented educational system. Somewhere among these polar positions I assume there are those who feel that the protests are often over genuine issues, that the schools are in need of some institutional reform, and that school personnel should develop more humanistic approaches to students.

One way to react thoughtfully is to re-examine what we mean by American civic education, since this is the process by which we expect youth to enter the political system. Civic education in a nation's schools will obviously be shaped by the dominant political credo and power relationships of society, as well as its prevailing image of the roles to be played by various citizen groups. Such civic education cannot be uniform throughout a nation's history. It must undergo significant changes as the nation moves from one sociopolitical era to another and adapts its formulation of citizen roles to those changing sociopolitical conditions.

Civic education does not refer simply to what is formally taught about the political system in the schools but includes four interrelated elements: the *classroom content of civic education*, expressed primarily in textbooks and curriculum materials; the *process of instruction*, represented by the modes of teaching and the basic student-teacher interactions; the *organization and administration of the school itself*, which represents the daily political world experienced by the school student; and the *relations of the school to the local community*, which expresses to students the status of the school bureaucracy in terms of its relation to outside political authorities and interests.

Historically, American civic education has featured a content expressing constitutional and democratic ideals, plus a way of conducting school life that has clearly set our civic education apart in content, process, and school organization from the civic education systems of nineteenth-century aristocratic regimes or twentieth-century totalitarian systems. Within this over-all democratic orientation, however, American civic education has maintained rather different models of "good citizenship" for different school populations, according to certain assumptions about citizen roles in our society that have been at the heart of our civic education tradition but have not been expressed openly.

Let me explain what I mean by this. As I read American constitutional law, political history, and social norms, we have had for most of our history a threefold conception and political treatment of our population. First have been the *leading elites,* the local and national spokesmen for business, agricultural, labor, religious, and civic interests who have played a dominant, though competitive, insider's role in our formal and informal governmental system.

Second is the *general citizenry,* an expanding base of population that has been brought steadily into middle-class economic status and civic participation, the 60 per cent of our adult population who join voluntary associations, vote in presidential elections, and feel a basic sense of civic identification with the American political system.

Finally, there are what I call the *unincorporated,* some of them temporary groups, such as the new immigrants as they arrived and American women until they achieved suffrage. Some of the unincorporated are relatively permanent groups, however, such as the American black population and the continuing poor. The basic feature of the unincorporated is that they have been blocked in various ways from access to the mainstream of American political and social life.

My reason for setting out these definitions, which I think most political scientists and historians would accept, is that American civic education has had rather separate systems for socializing each of these three groups as they entered the public schools. This fact bears on our current dilemmas with civic education and student unrest.

During the first century of our national life—the pre-industrial era from the 1770s through the 1860s—private and church elementary schools and private high school academies gave the elite an education in American constitutional principles. They were presented with an ideal of the rational citizen who pursued the public interest in an era of limited government and of political predominance by private business and agricultural interests.

When public elementary schools were established in northern states in the 1840s and 1850s, partially in response to the demands of workingmens' groups and liberal reformers, and partially to meet the needs of new factory owners for well-trained and well-socialized workers, the textbooks and teaching processes in these public schools presented the children of the general citizenry with civic lessons reciting the freedom and benefits afforded by republican government and outlining the duty of good citizens to support American institutions. In this era, of course, there was virtually no public education for the black or the poor.

The second major period of American civic education runs from the rise of the comprehensive high school and of expanded elementary education in the 1870s down through the 1950s. This was the industrial age, with the development of an industrial-capitalist economy, mass immigration from Southern and Eastern Europe, the institutionalization of racial segregation in both South and North, American overseas enterprises in the Far East and Latin America, efforts at progressive and then New Deal reforms, participation in two world wars, and general nationalization of the American political system. Now, children of the general citizenry and even segments of the unincorporated population were steadily brought into the public schools for socialization. The general theory of civic education they received was one of Americanization, the melting-pot concept that stressed the understanding and acceptance of American ideals and institutions, along with a concept that public policy is made by the equitable adjustment of divergent social, economic, and cultural interests, primarily through voting and the political party system.

If one looks at the histories of American education that tell us about this era of public schools from 1870 to the 1950s, what is remarkable is that they say little or nothing about student protest within the schools. There is much discussion about competing educational philosophies and theories of school organization, and some connection of these matters to the larger social and political conflicts within this period. There is even a little discussion of nationality, religious, and racial tensions in the schools. What is not mentioned is the fact that the American high school already was registering a growing tension between basic democratic ideals and two operating realities of American education: an authority-centered system of teaching and school governance and an unreal and distorted content-presentation of American social and political realities.

During the past few months, as part of our work on current student protests, several research assistants have gone through newspaper accounts of school conflict from the 1870s to the present, using primarily the New York *Herald,* the New York *Tribune,* and the New York *Times.* What we have found is a steady stream of serious student protests throughout this period—strikes, boycotts, sit-ins, demonstrations, and the like. The issue categories are remarkably similar to those of our own time. There were frequent riots, strikes, and boycotts over racial questions, primarily in Northern schools where white students, usually supported by their parents, resisted the introduction of even small numbers of black students into white high schools. There were also riots between black and white students coexisting uneasily in school against the backdrop of open discrimination in the outside society. Cities like Chicago, New York City, and Gary, Indiana, had recurring upheavals over these problems throughout this era.

Student representation and participation in school decision-making was another constant source of discontent. In the early 1900s, students struck and boycotted to win the creation in public high schools of what was called the General Organization, a forerunner of student councils. This provided for general school elections and gave representatives of student organizations in the school some powers, with faculty members in close watch, to manage various athletic, social, and extracurricular activities in the high schools. Once the general organizations were established, students engaged in further strikes over lunchroom policies, a share in the setting of student discipline, and arbitrary actions by school administrators. During this period, however, there seemed to be no efforts by students to win participation in curriculum decisions.

School histories also have neglected a continuing current of student protest over political control of student beliefs and expressions by school authorities. During World War I, many school systems put in rules requiring high school students to pledge their loyalty in writing to local, state, and national governments as a requirement for graduation.

In the early 1930s, hundreds of students in various schools refused to sign such pledges, and eventually the requirement was repealed. During the middle 1930s, one-day peace strikes with outdoor rallies and downtown peace marches were held in hundreds of high schools across the country to protest the spread of fascism and to pledge refusal to fight in any foreign wars. Later in the Thirties, antiwar speakers were allowed, as a result of student protests, to speak at antiwar assemblies on April "Peace Day" in many high schools throughout the country.

We found similar student protests involving educational issues, principally strikes to protest the firing or failure to renew contracts of well-liked teachers. Often these were teachers who had annoyed school authorities for their pro-student practices. There were also lawsuits, demonstrations, and even strikes over school dress codes—to protest the banning of long hair for boys in 1914, knickers for girls in the 1920s, mustaches and beer jackets for boys in the 1930s, slacks for girls in the 1940s, and bans on dungarees in the 1950s. Finally, when industrial conflict swept through American communities, clashes between children of strikers and nonstrikers often took place in the schools, as well as various clashes involving different nationality and religious groups.

The point of taking this time to record a forgotten chapter in American school history is that such protests were early signals that there were important gaps between democratic ideals and school civic education practices, that deep racial cleavages in American communities were bound to spill over into the schools. It also indicates that American historians and social commentators tend to play down conflict in our history. They either deny it existed or minimize the need to study it in order to produce a civic education that has democratic ideals and school power relationships in closer harmony. This tendency also produces materials that lead students to expect harmony rather than conflict in adult political life.

The public school is caught up in what is clearly a larger attack upon institutions that is sweeping American society—affecting our churches, universities, corporations, political parties, and governmental agencies —as well as all industrial societies and many of the developing nations, also. We have entered an age when the legitimacy and respect customarily accorded authority and institutions by the citizenry has been questioned.

Beyond the currents of student protest that are basically anti-institutional and part of the larger social scene, are there aspects of American civic education itself that may be stimulating student discontent in the late 1960s? There is a good deal in the literature of professional educators and social scientists that suggests that this may be so.

Despite many curricular manifestos since 1916 calling for realistic and venturesome discussions of American political life and its problems, civic education today is still overwhelmingly Mickey Mouse.

Professor Robert Hess of Stanford University, co-author of a study of political learning in the schools, wrote recently in the *Harvard Educational Review* that "the schools have contributed to divisions within the society by teaching a view of the nation and its political processes which is incomplete and simplistic, stressing values and ideals but ignoring social realities." The main type of civic education, Hess continues, stresses character-building and respect for rules and authority, undercutting the creation of "urgency about change and the solution of problems." Civic education emphasizes the vote and minimizes other political processes. It also creates "distaste in children for conflict and division within the society," thereby fostering avoidance of "unpleasant social and political facts." Finally, constitutional principles are taught abstractly, with little attention to concrete situations illustrating the costs to individuals and society in the violation of such rights by government or political groups.

Furthermore, as a study by Professor Edgar Litt shows, we are still teaching effective political education primarily to the children of the elite. Litt studied the civics texts and curricular presentations in three communities in greater Boston. "In the working class community," he reports, "civic education offers training in the basic democratic procedures without stressing political participation or the . . . view of conflict and disagreement as [being] indigenous to the political system." Politics is presented primarily in terms of "formal governmental institutions working in harmony for the benefit of citizens." Political participation in this community is quite low.

In the second community, a lower-middle-class school system, Litt found more stress on how government institutions work and on the responsibilities of citizenship, but "not on the dynamics of public decision-making." Formal political participation in this community is higher than the first, but primarily in terms of formal activities.

Finally, in the third community, an "affluent and politically vibrant community," Litt found civic education materials and teaching that provide extensive insights into how politics really works and how the system is used by those who seek to advance their interests.

If Litt's study in the Boston area is typical, much of the high school's civic education is geared to making working-class youngsters political drones, middle-class children citizen-soldiers, and upper-class children the sophisticated political elite taught how to manage the society.

The way in which many classrooms and schools are administered and students are governed in the largest segment of their daily life has also been found to create a growing gap between the democratic ideals students are taught and the authority system they experience in schools. We have seen that many other institutions of our society have been constitutionalized by judicial de-

cisions during the past few decades: corporations in
their dealing with workers; labor unions in their obligation to protect the liberty, equality, and due-process
rights of those they represent in industry; and private
universities and churches when they take disciplinary
action against their members.

Yet it is common in many high schools for students
to be denied the right to express and circulate dissent-
ing views on matters of school policy when such does
not suit the administration; for administrations to cen-
sor school newspapers on matters of political content;
for dress codes to be promulgated that deny legitimate
and reasonable modes of self-presentation; for students
to have their desks, lockers, or persons searched by
school officials without any attempt to apply the essential principles of constitutional privacy; for meaningful
forms of due process to be denied students when serious
disciplinary action is taken against them; and for student government to be tightly controlled by the school
administration through rules as to who is eligible to
run, what issues can be considered, and what decisions
require faculty or administration approval. In addition,
black students in many white schools can document
the fact that they are treated in a stricter fashion when
they break rules or seek school privileges than when
white students are involved.

Obviously, these practices represent the traditional
view that high school students are essentially immature
adolescents who have neither the intellectual nor emotional readiness to share responsibly in school decision-
making. There is much to suggest that this view, whatever its validity in the past, badly underestimates
today's youth aged fifteen to nineteen. And when stu-

dents hear democratic messages in their classes but experience autocratic treatment in the decisions that shape their lives, the clear message of our era is that such treatment will not go unchallenged for long.

The final ingredient of current civic education, the school-community relationship, poses a series of problems today. In ghetto communities, black parents and students are seeking a larger voice in the shaping of school policy, claiming the same rights for neighborhoods within the city that suburban and exurban parents have in their communities. Former United States Commissioner of Education Harold Howe noted that what is being sought is direct involvement, and this cannot be achieved without "some transfer of power, some award of discretion about how the funds for public education shall be put to use."

Another problem with the school-community relationship involves the belief of many students, joined by a wide variety of spokesmen from industry and social science as well as educators, that high school civic education ought to involve students more actively in meaningful civic and social service work in local communities. If these are Mickey Mouse work-study programs, they will be—and have been—rejected by students. But there is considerable hunger for greater involvement by students in the real world during their high school years, and denial of this involvement creates a sense of wasteful imprisonment among some of the best high school students we have.

To mention only one more problem, children in white schools today receive far too little education about black people than they desperately need to get. It is white students who really need courses on Afro-

American history, culture, and politics. After all, black people know all about the white world—its rules, messages, and values are broadcast endlessly throughout the society and its culture. But most white children are given so little information in school about black culture and have such limited social contacts with black children that we are in danger of bringing up still another generation of whites that will lack the basic knowledge and understanding of black people and their aspirations. If our civic education continues in such a vacuum, how can we expect to move race policies in our country where they must go if we are to achieve racial justice, and with it, racial peace?

My general conclusion is that a significant part—though by no means all—of current student unrest stems from antidemocratic teaching and administration within our schools and from school-aggravated tensions from the larger society over issues such as racial conflict and political dissent.

Taking this view, I do not think that it will be easy for any school administration or city government that is inclined to do so to put the lid of forcible control back on the schools. The protests are too deep and too widespread for this policy to work, short of stationing policemen at short intervals in every school corridor. Even if such interventions could work, I would oppose them vigorously, since I believe that fundamental reforms in the content, process, and government of our schools is essential if American society is to cope effectively with the pressures of social change.

Of course there is a need for order and structure. But when justice and participation are provided, order will emerge in that context. Where it does not emerge naturally, discipline should be applied and will then be widely respected.

What keeps us then from moving to a new and more effective form of civic education today? To some extent, of course, continued divisions in the larger society over the Vietnam War, racial justice, and the new forms of political participation make any sweeping new program of civic education difficult. When consensus is shattered and conflict is high in the society, the tendency for established institutions is to coast, waiting for the new consensus to be available for installation.

But even more than this, the fact is that the way the American public school is legally, administratively, and professionally organized makes it one of the most conservative and rigid institutions in our society. This is true for many complex, historical reasons, but its reality has been attested by study after study examining how long it usually takes for changes to be instituted in curriculum, teacher training, school administration, or school-community relations.

Yet it is precisely the absence of time for leisurely change that is the central political fact of our era. Neither the race conflict nor the intergenerational conflict can be postponed.

Since elaborate prescriptions are out of the question, let me at least discuss three important approaches that I think belong high on our priority list.

First, very few of the things that need to be done with civic education, or with public schools in general for that matter, come at discount prices. Quality schools for the ghettos, more and better trained teachers and teacher aides, work-study programs for students, effective use of new technology and instructional systems, and better curriculum materials, all cost well beyond the $35.5 billion that we now spend. But we could do much by using the school time we *now* have, and the paid time of teachers, administrators, and the like to design new programs, try them, and perfect them through experience. The task is to *stop doing* what we do now through ritual, fear, or outmoded laws and practices.

Second, school administrators, teachers, and governmental officials concerned with education will have to learn new modes of behavior in facing what promise to be continuing intergenerational and interracial conflicts in the schools. I have been greatly impressed by work that is being done in a project on "Conflict Intervention in Secondary Schools," headed by Professor Mark Chesler, a social psychologist at the University of Michigan. Chesler and his associates are working with a number of school districts across the country that are experiencing serious school disruptions. The position taken by this project is that such conflicts cannot be avoided, suppressed, or bargained away, even by enormous concessions by school administrators. Moreover, given the fact that interracial and intergenerational conflicts arise because of larger conflicts in American society and the existing status of schools as rigid, authority-centered institutions, Chesler argues that what is needed is expert training and experience in conflict-resolution for all the relevant parties to school confrontations—the students, teachers, parents, administrators, government officials, and community group leaders.

Third, we must transform the four basic elements of American civic education into far more participative processes than they have been in the past. This means opening up to student participation everything from a voice in the creation of new curriculum and in the management of new technological systems of instruction to the making of basic decisions about the rules of school government and the links between school and community.

I think the era of "top down reform" in American education is over, and its record during the 1950s and 1960s does not suggest that many tears need to be shed for its passing. "Teacher-proof materials," "university-savant projects for underprivileged minds," "USOE force-fit experiments with systems-analysis and computerized instruction"—these are stories of flawed conceptions and failed projects. In their place, I think we must substitute models of decentralized curriculum-making and experimentation with new forms of learning. The current Triple-T Program of USOE, on "Training the Teachers of Teachers" seems to me a step in just the right direction. It calls for "parity relations" among university schools of education, university arts and sciences faculties, school systems, and community spokesmen to develop programs for giving prospective teachers the intellectual, professional, and civic skills to be relevant in the classroom of the 1970s. Here is the model of cooperative relations around which the American school might help to bring us back to a new sense of local and national community. My own center has begun to do this on an "in-service" basis with a nearby school system, and it is a venture that should be going on in hundreds of American communities today.

This policy of increased participation applies just as much to teachers, parents, and community spokesmen as to students. Even apart from crisis management and conflict resolution, school administrators must develop far more sharing of decisions than has been the rule of public education to this date.

Participation is not a magic formula for extracting gold from rough ore, but all we have to do to keep our perspective is to consider the alternative—a level of interracial and intergenerational conflict that will transform our society into armed camps and guerrilla warfare.

It is easy to be swept along by emotional cries of "no appeasement" or "nonnegotiable demands." But if either of those extreme positions remains substantially unmodified in the coming years, our school systems are headed for disaster.

Facing the
Issues

William L. Smith

CLEVELAND'S EXPERIMENT IN MUTUAL RESPECT

So FAR, the United States has overcome, with reasonable success, whatever it has regarded as a crisis in public education. Sputnik is one example. When the Russians orbited the first satellite, Americans responded by demanding that science and mathematics be upgraded in the public schools. This outcry led to additional course offerings and large-scale curriculum experimentation in these fields and, eventually, to better prepared students. The Sputnik crisis was thus ended, and we, as a nation, set the matter aside and went on to other things.

We are a crisis-oriented society. We bring together our mammoth resources and manpower; we address ourselves to the problem; we develop the solutions; and we put the mechanism in operation to get the job done. We never stop to think that the job cannot be done in a short period of time because we are not a humble nation. We are an arrogant society. Our arrogance is

WILLIAM L. SMITH is former Executive Director of The PACE Association of Cleveland.

based upon the bootstrap, self-made, rugged individualistic nature of our existence. This is our tradition, our
heritage, and our national pride. We have made it, as
a people, against tremendous odds.

We have moved to the point where we are an instant
action society. We expect instant coffee, instant TV
dinners, instant headache relief, instant information
retrieval systems, and so forth.

Yet problems that are people problems do not fit
these instant systems, and the sooner we accept this,
the more effective will be our efforts. It is unusually
difficult for us to accept the fact that we cannot im-
mediately accomplish what we set out to do in a most
expeditious manner.

One of these problems that defies an instant solution
is the problem of urban education.

The heart of the present crisis in public education is
the realization that the system has failed a major segment of the population. This fact became obvious to the
general public when the nation took official cognizance
of poverty amidst affluence and when minority groups
began to assert their civil rights and demand a full
share in political and economic opportunity.

Yet this failure was the most intractable crisis in the
urban setting all along. Why, then, did it take so long
for it to become public knowledge? There appear to be
many reasons for this, but the main reason is that
minority children were different from the rest. Educators did not respect them enough to think them
worthy of attention. They were simply written off as
not being able. They did not represent a crisis; therefore, the problems of dealing with them were hidden
from society.

In the past, schools were viewed as having the specific function of transmitting the cultural heritage so that the child could take his place as a contributing member of society. As a mirror of society, the school provided the formal, graduated learning experiences which prepared the child for this mission. Society viewed the school as its formal tool for perpetuating its values and traditions.

Since the purposes and intentions of public education are based upon what society values and the available data about the student, no new mandates could be issued for education.

But this is not the case today. There is now a disparity between what is intended and what is going on in the schools. We know there is a human crisis and there is the need for a new mandate regarding the mission of education.

To date, there is little agreement on what has caused the failure of the schools. One extreme says that the failure to learn lies with the learner. The other extreme takes the position that this failure rests with the school system. But never has much consideration been given to the idea that the educational crisis is caused by the failure of our society to provide the realistic value orientation for the mission of the schools as they relate to the world today.

There is an abundance of evidence that indicates that those who are not directly involved in urban education view that scene with great disdain. They tend to be appalled by what is seen, read, and heard. But they are also somewhat intentionally removed from the immediate crisis because they rationalize that it is someone else's problem and does not directly affect them. We are all guilty in some respect for harboring this thinking whether we acknowledge it or not.

We are quick to blame because we do not see ourselves having a charged responsibility for the situation. This is not to say that we do not have a solution, nor that we do not want the responsibility. But since someone else has that responsibility, it is sufficient for us to look at what is being done and be concerned, but critical.

I know it is difficult for us to redirect our thinking from provincial isolationism and self-achievement to the concepts of metropolitanism and shared responsibility. But it would be at least a little easier if those in the suburbs realized that they were not as isolated from the inner city as they thought. The first principle of the system theory states that what affects one part inevitably affects all parts. Therefore, what affects the child in the inner city today will affect the child in the outer city tomorrow and the child in the suburbs the day after tomorrow. However, its residue may already be there. In 1960, the Labor Department said that 1 child in 3 could be labeled "disadvantaged." It forecast that, by 1970, 1 child in every 2 could be considered disadvantaged. Already these statistics have proved very real. What then will the next decade produce?

The present preoccupation with the disadvantaged has not really diverted critics of public education from concluding that the total system is incapable of providing an excellent education for a diverse student population. The student movements coming from the predominantly white, middle-class sections of the country indicate that the mission of fundamental educational reform is not for the poor and black alone but for all children. It is simply that the greatest number with the greatest and most immediate need can be found in the core of the city. This is where most of the attention is presently directed.

In September, 1965, I was the new principal of a junior high school in such an area. It was the largest junior high school in Ohio and had the reputation of being the toughest in the state.

I opened school that fall with 2 new assistant principals, a new administrative intern, 2 new guidance counselors, and 27 new teachers. We and our colleagues were responsible for 2,500 children in a forty-four-year-old building with a capacity for 1,850 children.

There were 170 children new to the school system. The great influx of new residents who had settled in the area during the past few years had drastically changed the composition and attitudes of the community. Many of the children who attended our school and their parents had a total distrust and even an open contempt for the school and its staff.

The building was still operating with the original low candlepower lighting. Most of the classrooms had the original, often damaged, stationary desks. The 7 exterior doors were so old that a shake and a tug from the outside would release the panic bar. Any trespasser could walk in—and usually did. That year we experienced at least 1 fire, 10 locker thefts, and 3 fights of mammoth proportion every week.

I venture to say that you can find these same conditions existing in many urban schools today, if not in toto then in some proportion. Usually, these schools will be labeled failures because the odds are overwhelm-

ingly stacked against them. The elements conducive to
learning are not there. Yet, failure does not have to
be the inevitable conclusion.

In our own case in 1965, we decided that it was
imperative to develop a set of priorities to cope with
our situation. Our first priority was to recognize that
we had problems that looked insurmountable but could
be overcome. We were firmly convinced the evidence
indicated that when the attitude of the teacher changed,
most often the attitude of the child changed, that as the
child and parent developed more positive attitudes
toward themselves and the school, the achievement
level would rise.

In brief, the operational design of the school was
built around two concepts: justification and respect.
We employed the principle that one teaches by example. If one could not justify his actions in terms of
the school's established criteria, then it should not be
done. This applied to administrators, pupils, and teachers. Administrators could not assume, prejudge, or
attempt to falsely defend either a teacher's or a pupil's
behavior until all evidence was considered carefully.
It became essential that both the teacher and the pupil
be granted a fair hearing in whatever situation occurred. Administrators discovered they had to listen
with an open mind, regardless of their own personal
impressions, to what the child and the teacher were
saying. We practiced the principle that no child or
teacher should ever leave an office feeling his concerns
had not been heard or that there was not an understanding of these expressed concerns by an administrator.

This is very difficult to do when there are vast numbers of cases referred each day, but it must be done. I stress this point because it was the basis from which all other action flowed. When there is a high turnover of staff, as there is in most inner-city schools today, and there are overcrowded conditions, as there are in some schools, the instability of the situation makes it nearly impossible to develop consistency of behavior among pupils and teachers.

It takes time for new, young, insecure teachers, regardless of their commitment, to gain confidence in themselves and recognize that the behavior of a child is not personally threatening to their position of authority and that the inner-city child's behavior is not atypical of the behavior of a child in any school. Only then can he develop an understanding of the needs of the children and the techniques and methodology necessary to teach the child the subject, rather than the subject to the child.

It takes even more time for young, insecure children, struggling to develop a concept of themselves while being bombarded by negative environmental forces, to learn to accept the teacher as an authority figure who is sensitive to their needs.

Until this is done, too much time will be spent on disciplinary problems. Too little time will be spent on the educational needs of the children.

In 1965—in that big, tough junior high school—we found that the administrator must act as a mediator for both the pupil and the teacher. Both were experiencing culture clashes. It was necessary for the teacher, first, to understand the framework in which the child operated and, second, to reduce the stultifying effect of the negative environment on the child's conceptual development.

Culturally disadvantaged children learn very early that they are caught up in the cycle of poverty. They suspect that society rejects them. And, of course, they are right. Rejection breeds self-doubt and self-blame. The child grows to view himself as worthless in his relation to others. A poor self-concept produces aggression and aberrant behavior.

Many of our pupils felt that the school was naïve, apathetic, or dishonest in its refusal to come to grips with their obvious problems and handicaps. They often reacted with aggression and aberrant behavior. We found that success in meeting educational needs and obtaining educational objectives is affected by the extent to which those basic needs are either satisfied or ignored.

Our teachers found that adapting methods, materials, and activities to the experience of the children really begins with their own creativity, their high expectation for each pupil, and the realization that inner-city children can learn. The teacher became the meaningful and direct link between the pupil and the cultures of the real world. He acted as a model for general behavioral patterns and values of the dominant culture.

In conducting learning experiences, the importance of the classroom teacher as mediator between the disadvantaged pupil and his environment is great. The teacher has to provide more explanation, more interpretation, more encouragement and reward.

Probably even more significant is the fact that our teachers could never become discouraged with small gains in evaluating the learning experience of our children. There were times when teachers wondered if the actions and attitudes of pupils indicated that they did not want to be educated. But, when teachers remembered that these pupils were products of a background that had conditioned them one way, that they had never really had a choice between actions and attitudes that support education and actions and attitudes that reject education, they gave them this choice.

There are far too many children in urban schools today who do not learn as well as they might because they simply are not clear about what their lives are for and what is worth working for. They have not yet found a meaning for their lives and are therefore unable or unwilling to marshal up their full intellectual resources for use in the crucial game of living. Unless those charged with the responsibility to provide the setting and structure in which the child can experience success, realize his own worth, and be equipped to make choices from the alternatives available to him, there is no need for an educational system.

If it is the administrators' and teachers' function to provide a climate for the children to learn in, then it remains the system's responsibility to provide the proper climate for the administrators and teachers. Finally, it is the responsibility of all citizens to provide the climate for the school system. To provide this climate, we must be involved in the process.

It is quite easy for one to become involved in the process of destroying the system, whether intentionally or unintentionally. But the basis of our society is founded on the precept that institutions are necessary, that they must have a discipline, and that they must

serve the welfare of society. It becomes unrealistic to
think of not having a system of some kind.

What then does this mean for each citizen? How can
we involve ourselves in the reformation of the urban
educational system as an outside power source and be
acceptable as anything other than an unofficial lay
board of education?

For the past six years in the city of Cleveland, an
organized group of citizens has committed itself to
share the blame for public education in the urban setting especially. The group is called the PACE Association—Programs for Action by Citizens in Education.

What they have shown is the need for citizens' organizations to accept evidence that something does not
work and to pursue other possibilities as systematically
as possible without pushing panic buttons and without
dismissing the educational enterprise as being worthless.

PACE is an organization of 40 trustees—black and
white, urban and suburban. No one on the payroll of
a school system or on a board of education is eligible.
It is totally independent of any school system or other
institutions, with the prime responsibility of addressing
itself (1) to work with existing organizations to review
its own plan for action and help carry out its recom-
mendations, (2) to foster a climate of opinion which
demands quality elementary and secondary education
for all Cuyahoga County children, and (3) to provide
a badly needed countrywide mechanism for the many
citizens who want to work in the best interest of all
the schools.

PACE has assumed the role of a catalytic agent for
change. It has been viewed as a broker by a few, as a
gadfly by some, as an interloper by others, and as

a means for the development of high-risk experimental programs by many.

Regardless of how it is viewed by institutions, it is the one independent citizens' organization that can evaluate what is going on in the schools. It has the facilities and manpower to orchestrate and coordinate community services to education.

What is of real importance is the PACE approach to organizing. The group redefined urban education to include the Greater Cleveland area and recognized that there are different needs in different parts of the greater city. PACE accepted the reality that persons most intimately involved in particular schools have their finger on basic and instructional needs that must be met before societal needs can be met.

PACE has made evaluation a legitimate and positive external review.

There is a dramatic need for a positive environment within the city schools if we hope that children will emerge as productive and effective citizens. This will not happen overnight because it is a people problem. Schools must be able to deal directly with problems that these children confront in their daily lives. They must deal with the emotional responses of children. They cannot do this in the urban setting alone.

There must be involvement by all citizens. Educators are not able to do it alone. The mission and role of education in our society are not to be determined by educators. Educators bring the skills to help implement what is decided. The mission and role of educators are decided by an involved and informed citizenry, motivated not out of fear or reaction but from a rational set of positive steps that the mind and evidence say we can do something about.

Facing the Issues

David Mallery

VOICES INSIDE THE BELEAGUERED SCHOOL

IN A RECENT and organized confrontation between students, teachers, and administrators, a school principal complained: "It looks as if we can't make any moves right now on our own. We see the need for change, for humanizing things, for breaking through old structures. And we're just finding ways to do it, along with the determination and backing to do it. But now when we introduce any of these things, the kids reject them. 'We have to fight for these things,' they say. 'We have to wrest them from the administration. It's no good if they just grant us something.'"

There was a sudden, surprising silence after the principal had finished. Then a young man, a junior in college who was very critical of his own school experiences, spoke up: "If what you say is right, then we're all sunk. I don't mean just the schools. All of us. The whole society."

There was another silence. Then a girl, a high school

DAVID MALLERY is Director of Studies, National Association of Independent Schools.

senior, turned around in her chair to look at the man who had spoken first: "It just can't be that way. I guess we can't afford to let it be that way. Isn't there some kind of partnership, some way of working together, some way where human beings can get together in a school and do something better than fight for victories over each other?"

The three who had spoken—and the twenty-seven others in the room—were determined to believe that "there was still time." The principal's comment was the farthest any of them got from this belief, and he himself had spoken in the eager hope that what he said did not close all the doors, that "partnership" had something to do with a real possibility, a real necessity.

When I am out in the schools talking with students, teachers, and administrators, I sometimes feel like yelling out this question: Doesn't anybody talk to anybody else around here?

And I do ask it when I can, when the talk falls heavily into Us and Them. Them is any other group: hippies, students, student leaders, old-pro teachers, the Parent-Teacher Association, the school administration, the school board, the math and science teacher, the police, the whites, the blacks. But when it's really frightening is when Us and Them refers simply to adults and students.

Yet in any group of Them, I often hear an idea, a grievance, or a hope which echoes loudly something I heard an hour before from Us. Or I hear a fear from Them that would be helpful and reassuring to a fearful Us. Or a flash of compassion in Us that would surprise Them. Or a common aim about curriculum or school morale or individual style which both Us and

Them have real convictions about, if they only talked to each other enough to discover.

Listen to the students:

A SIXTEEN-YEAR-OLD BOY: I sometimes have the feeling that everything we do has been done before—it's all spelled out, printed, carried through the years, along with the answer book.

A SEVENTEEN-YEAR-OLD GIRL: It seems as if there's nothing for us to do but say, Oh hell, all right. The curriculum planners, the publishers, the packagers, the administrators, and the teachers have the courses all mapped out. Our own teacher is so gung ho that he has a whole lot more of his own that we get. You get the feeling that there's nothing left that can be ours, nothing for us to do but chew it all and swallow it, and then say "I did it. What now?"

MORE YOUNG VOICES: "We need some options." "We want a say in what's offered." "If there could be a course maybe in psychology . . ." ". . . in political science . . ." ". . . in 'Awareness' . . ." ". . . in Dissent . . ." and, with rising intensity and frequency, ". . . in black history, black identity, black consciousness, black painting, black writing . . ."

Actually it is rather recent news that students think the curriculum is worth attacking or even discussing. Many still do not. The action in school, let alone outside school, is someplace else. But for some very astute young people—some loaded with As and IQ and some not—the curriculum is clearly worth talking about, even fighting about. A lot of students are sick of the word "relevance" in talk about the school. Yet I have heard no student who is sick of the meaning of "relevance." As one boy said, "Something should happen in some class or course we're taking that has to do with *me*—what I'm thinking or feeling or worrying about or seeing in the world."

But the students are not alone.

An English teacher put his head in his hands with embarrassment when he described how seven years ago he had used a unit for eleventh-grade English on Ethical Concerns of Young People. "I made the list of the concerns!" he moaned. "I thought I knew what they were. The kids were nice about it—they 'discussed' politely. They wouldn't today. It's lucky I found out before they did that it was foolish—actually insulting —for me to mimeograph those concerns without any checking with them as to what the real ones were. I was twenty-two then—near their age—it seemed easy. I'm older now—more separated from the kids in age and less separated from them in understanding, because I've been hearing a thing or two in the last few years."

At a regional teachers meeting, where the curriculum and relevancy were getting worked over, one man spoke up: "I had a lot of revelations about education when I was in college—great ideas that meant a lot to me. Yet I'm locked in a school battling it out with apathy and *Julius Caesar* and *Silas Marner*. Nobody made me do this. I guess there are a lot of forces inside us, when we've come up through school with a certain set of experiences, to make us fall back on them. But I know *better* than that, damn it!"

And how about the administrators? Nobody ever told them that school had to be barren of feeling, of connections with the students' lives. It just somehow got that way.

One of the most provocative and admired school principals in the country wrote this fall in a professional magazine for school administrators that schools should "put student protest into the curriculum. This may be the most effective way of handling protest. Students should be studying and talking about the most important issues of this decade: Can democracy work? What are the limits of dissent? Is civil disobedience ever justified? How can you use student power for constructive ends?"

And how about parents? They are the only group everybody blames when they talk about change in the schools. There remain plenty of communities that want to run the librarian out of towns if he hands out *The Catcher in the Rye.* But even in the community that just ran out its librarian, surely there are more than a few parents who are pleased when students come home newly alive to something they have studied or talked about in school. Many a parent rejoices to see his child caring deeply about anything that happens in school, feeling personally about it, not just working through the routine with apathy or, more recently, with rebelliousness. Ask the parent of the overprivileged suburban kid driving grimly toward the Ivy League over mountains of words and numbers who comes suddenly on something in the curriculum that relates to him. Ask the parent of an inner-city teen-ager—on the verge of dropping out because nothing in school has anything to do with him—who suddenly writes something, sees a film, paints a picture, gets into a study or discussion that awakens his sense of himself and the world. These parents can talk to school boards just as loudly as the community book burners can and with more emotion behind their talk.

What can we do with this student-teacher-administrator-parent ferment while there's still time?

We can still be human beings together. We—the educator and community leader, the tenth grader and the math teacher, the student activist and the faculty conservative, the anti-PTA father and the committee-organizing mother—can keep listening to each other and working together.

As one classroom teacher said: "My God, we're locked in there as human beings together, encountering each other for thousands of hours. Something important should be happening."

One "something important" is surely the experience of partnership between students and adults—the spirit the principal, the college student, and the high school girl were groping for in the conversation quoted at the beginning of this paper. I am beginning to hear about these "partnership experiences" around the country:

—A three-day retreat with administrators, teachers, parents, and students—the students chosen because they were on the verge of dropping out of high school.

—A city school where the student-teacher-administrator planning group achieved such a precious morale and action program that the school was allowed to have its own vacation schedule while the rest of the city's schools followed a different citywide edict.

—A small community high school where students see a film like *David and Lisa* or *In the Heat of the Night* in the afternoon and their parents see it in the evening so that talk goes in the school's classrooms, far into the night, and back home at the breakfast table.

I am often heartened by these new efforts to have students and adults plan together on matters concerning them both. This produces its own turmoil as people speak out to each other regardless of status and age. But a partnership can emerge so that everyone has a stake in making the school a place where individuals can do something that seems to make some sense, individually and together.

The possibility of students and adults forming that "partnership" seems even greater when still another student's words are considered:

"There's too much asking the young people to have their say. This is just too easy on the adults and not interesting enough for us. Yesterday . . . a principal said, 'Now, let's let the young people say what's on their mind . . . and we'll keep quiet.' He meant to give us an opening. . . . But we're not going to sit there and tell our concerns while half the people in the room sit there and make no commitment themselves. We want to talk with you. We want to hear what your concerns are too. We want you to stick your necks out. Then we'll stick ours out. We don't want an audience for our concerns. We want to talk back and forth—all of us—together."

Facing the Issues

James M. Becker

A COURSE IN QUESTIONS WITHOUT ANSWERS

ALTHOUGH MANY INSTITUTIONS are involved in inducting the young into politics, schools represent the official, deliberate attempt of society to teach its members about government, political processes, and the proper role of individuals within the political system. Political education generally takes up a significant portion of the school curriculum; according to one estimate nearly one half of the school program in grades five to twelve is politically relevant.

Since so much time and money is spent on political education it would appear that this is an area the public strongly supports. It would also appear that it is a subject well worth the attention of scholars and likely to attract the interest of the concerned public as well. Yet such interest has been notably lacking. The reasons generally advanced for this lack of concern include: (1) the nonpolitical image schools seem to have, (2) the fact that politically relevant aspects of the over-all

JAMES M. BECKER is National Director of the School Services section of the Foreign Policy Association.

program are obscured by the many kinds of learning that go in schools, and (3) the difficulties associated with uncovering links between schools and government in a decentralized educational system.

Yet whatever explanations are given for this neglect, the situation is changing rapidly because of the present turmoil in American society, the increasing complexity of government, and the recent increasing interest of social scientists in schools. Several recent research studies have examined the school's role in political education, and it is becoming a more frequent topic for treatment in the popular journals.

The school's capacity to provide a continuing and extensive program in civic education is influenced by the resources—staff, leadership, instructional materials, physical facilities, and talent—available. It is also influenced by what leaders in the community, the political system, and the educational system expect of the schools.

What is taught in schools may, in part, reflect our national political values, but the schools are not thereby agencies of the national political system. They are, instead, primarily the agents of local social, economic, and political conditions, and their role is more often aimed at preserving those local conditions than concerning themselves with national problems.

Differing racial, religious, nationality, and regional groupings are common in our public schools. These groupings or blends of groupings may determine to a considerable extent what is emphasized in curriculum, in recruiting staff, and in general orientation.

Where there is a considerable mix of different groups and interests within the boundaries of a school district, teachers and administrators may resist group pressures in favor of the national or long-range view. But the presence of interest groups, organized politically, is likely to have considerable effect on the program of civic education. A variety of regional and local groups is also likely to have this effect. The school is not the only institution which respects differences among these groups, but it is more likely to be involved in preserving traditional patterns which reflect local orientations and interests.

In the past, education has not been much of a force for social change, especially where controversial values or deep-seated taboos were at stake. Yet it seems imperative that in such cases clear, analytical thinking and intelligent judgment are needed. Moving education from a relatively passive role to one of leadership in social change may be necessary if present demands for equality of opportunity and social justice are to be met.

This is a particularly difficult role for the schools. Their role as transmitters of knowledge may be troublesome enough, but their role as promoters of questions is almost certain to create conflicts with the ideals and images of the local or folk culture. Emphasis on scientific objectivity may also lead students to offend the folk culture.

As part of the democratic social order, schools are not in a position to propose solutions to social issues and indoctrinate students for their acceptance. However, they have a right and responsibility to engage in learning and rational inquiry and to help students develop sound judgment on social and political issues. Constructive social change can be encouraged by helping citizens learn how to seek answers to questions which they must be able and free to raise.

There are many obstacles in establishing such a role for the schools. Conflicts among interest groups provide richness and vigor in a free society, but they also make many educators wary of dealing with some of the most crucial social issues of our time. The sheer number of students and the wide range of abilities and backgrounds represented make it difficult to teach the search for truth in an open-ended, objective way. The traditional approaches and outlooks still prevalent in many schools work against full utilization of the results of research and experimentation in the social sciences.

Yet man's survival in modern society may depend in large part upon his being able to distinguish fact from fancy, myth from reality, superstition from scientific knowledge, and upon his ability to use intelligent and appropriate procedures in solving problems.

The question of what should be the content of school programs in the area of civic education has been a troublesome one. It is generally accepted that instruction in this area should enable the individual to understand and cope with politics in an intelligent manner. Judged by the state and local requirements regarding civic education, it is apparent that traditions, rituals, ceremonies, and the governmental structure receive major emphasis in most schools.

Usually, the content of civics instruction is likely to vary from grade level to grade level with emphasis on attitudes and values in the earlier grades, and more emphasis in the middle school years on information about the structure of government and the role of the citizen. In the high school years a more realistic appraisal of politics is likely to be emphasized, including awareness of the role of group and special interests in issues and processes. In short, the largest component of civic education is likely to emphasize information about the formal structure of government and the political process. More delicate and less formally organized are the elements of the program designed to inculcate proper attitudes and values.

The problem of selecting appropriate content, making it relevant to students, and educating teachers to effectively use it has been the focus of experimental programs in many areas of curriculum. Emerging from these numerous experimental programs is a new social studies emphasizing the need to judge programs on the basis of what the student is able to decide for himself. Instruction is being designed to improve the student's capabilities for doing something, rather than merely adding to his store of facts. What is being taught is an intellectual skill, not simply a recallable verbal response.

The new social studies is concerned with helping the child become a useful, independent citizen. It recognizes the knowledge explosion, and so it puts great emphasis on inquiry skills. Discovering and directed discussion are given great emphasis. Questioning, challenging, pointing out exceptions to generalizations, introducing new evidence are all part of the classroom strategy in the new social studies. It is also used frequently for another purpose: teaching students how to deal with value conflicts.

Assuming that all democratic societies try to align their laws and practices with their values, it is inevitable that in many issues contradictory values are involved and need to be resolved. Teaching students how to deal with public controversies involving conflicting values and conflicting policies would seem to be essential in our form of government. The purpose here is to teach not that there are easy answers but rather that these are open questions which constantly need clarification and redefinition as society changes and man refines his tools for analyzing society.

What is also required is more frequent and more informal interactions between students and teachers and opportunities for students to make connections between thinking and acting. Recognition of the quality and potential of student concerns and contributions should form a part of such efforts.

Community-service experience enables students to use and sharpen what they learn in the classroom. These experiences also motivate students to learn as well as promote social skills and a sense of social responsibility.

Society no longer lets the young stay naïve. Informed by the mass media, urged by parents and teachers to question, the students are more sensitive to the larger world than were previous generations.

Student discontent testifies that students are learning from parents, from the mass media, from participation in the politics and social movements of the society. The schools have not taught students much of what they have learned. In terms of their general information, they are better informed than previous generations. Their leaders identify with the concerns of other subcultures, black and white, which have been invisible and are now trying to be heard. To many of these young people a simple law-and-order approach to divisiveness and social turmoil is seen as a cover up for a middle class trying to keep the blacks and poor in the ghettos.

Students may turn out to be a major force within educational institutions for reforming the system. Accepting this challenge will not be easy. To deny it could be disastrous.

PARTICIPANTS*

DONALD C. AGNEW Director, Southern Association of Colleges and Schools

WILLIAM E. AMOS Chief, Division of Counseling and Test Development, Bureau of Employment Security, U.S. Department of Labor

JOHN ANDERSON, JR. President, Citizens Conference on State Legislatures

VERNE S. ATWATER President, Westinghouse Learning Corporation

MISS LYNN AUMENT National Congress of American Indians

GERALDINE BAGBY Administrative Assistant, Metropolitan School District of Washington Township

GEORGE H. BAIRD Educational Research Council of America

* The following accepted invitations but were unable to attend: The Rev. Ralph D. Abernathy, Director, Southern Christian Leadership Conference; Lyle W. Ashby, Executive Secretary, National Education Association; Mrs. Bruce B. Benson, President, League of Women Voters; Lowell A. Burkett, Executive Director, American Vocational Association; Calvin L. Crawford, Administrative Secretary, Middle States Association of Colleges and Secondary Schools; Sam English, Executive Director, National Indian Youth Council; Edwin Fenton, Carnegie Education Center, Carnegie-Mellon University; Francis Fox, Chairman, D. C. Heath and Company; Robert W. Haigh, Vice President, Xerox Educational Division; Ralph E. Hall, Executive Director, American Veterans Association, National Headquarters; Harry J. Hogan, Counsel, Special Subcommittee on Education; Leon Jaworski, Attorney; John F. Jennings, Counsel, General Subcommittee on Education; Evron M. Kirkpatrick, Executive Director, American Political Science Association; Col. William G. McDonald, Administrative Officer, National Commission on the Causes and Prevention of Violence; Roy S. Padilla, Acting Secretary, League of United Latin American Citizens.

FRANK R. BARNETT President, National Strategy Information Center

DEVON BATES Executive Director, Citizenship Education Clearing House

JAMES M. BECKER National Director, School Services, Foreign Policy Association

A. EDGAR BENTON Vice Chairman, Denver School Board

ROBERT W. BLANCHARD Superintendent of Schools, Montclair, New Jersey

DICK T. BOBBITT, JR. Director, Educational Planning, RCA Educational Systems

NATHAN BRODSKY Acting Deputy Assistant Secretary for Education, Department of Defense

DAVID BRODY Anti-Defamation League

B. FRANK BROWN Director, Informational Services, I/D/E/A

DYKE BROWN Director, The Athenian School

STERLING W. BROWN President, National Conference of Christians and Jews

JAMES F. BUNTING Executive Director, National Council of Young Men's Christian Association

MRS. HERBERT P. CATLIN National Board of Young Women's Christian Association

THE REV. LUCIUS F. CERVANTES, S.J. Office of the Mayor, St. Louis, Missouri

TODD CLARK Educational Consultant, Constitutional Rights Foundation

RODNEY CLURMAN Education Department, National Association of Manufacturers

DANA M. COTTON Secretary/Treasurer, New England Association of Colleges and Schools

DON M. DAFOE Executive Secretary, Council of Chief State School Officers

SAMUEL DASH Vice Chairman, Criminal Law Section, American Bar Association

JAMES DENEEN Consultant, Public Education, Ford Foundation

RICHARD A. DERSHIMER Executive Officer, American Educational Research Association

CHARLES G. DOBBINS Executive Secretary, American Council on Education

HARRY DONOHUE Executive Assistant Director, Veterans of Foreign Wars, National Rehabilitation Service

NORMAN DRACHLER Superintendent of Schools, Detroit, Michigan

BERT H. EARLY Executive Director, American Bar Association

E. DANIEL ECKBERG Teacher, Minneapolis, Minnesota

CHRISTOPHER F. EDLEY Program Officer in Charge, Government and Law, Ford Foundation

ALEX ELSON Attorney

SHIRLEY ENGLE High School Curriculum Center in Government, Indiana University

RAYMOND ENGLISH Educational Research Council of America

MRS. AARON FISCHER Citizenship Education Clearing House

J. BLAINE FISTER Staff Associate for Public Education, National Council of the Churches of Christ

JOHN FITZWATER The United States Jaycees

MARCUS FOSTER Principal, Philadelphia, Pennsylvania

LAWRENCE H. FUCHS Vice President, Education Development Center

OTIS FULLER National Council of Boy Scouts

HERMAN GALLEGOS Executive Director, Southwest Council of La Raza Unida

JOHN F. GARDUNO American G.I. Forum of the U.S.

JOHN GIBSON Director, Lincoln Filene Center, Tufts University

CHARLES GUGGENHEIM Guggenheim Productions, Inc.

ROBERT HANVEY Professor, School of Education, Indiana University

WILLIAM G. HARLEY President, National Association of Educational Broadcasters

MERRILL F. HARTSHORN Executive Secretary, National Council for the Social Studies

THE HONORABLE BROOKS HAYS Executive Director, National Conference on Citizenship

MELVIN P. HELLER National Catholic Educational Association, Loyola University

FRANCIS H. HERRICK Secretary/Treasurer, Western College Association

ERMAN O. HOGAN National Urban League

ROY INNIS National Director, Congress of Racial Equality

ROBERT M. ISENBERG Associate Secretary, American Association of School Administrators

DOUGLAS KELLEY Executive Director, Encampment for Citizenship, Inc.

JAMES A. KELLY Education Director, Urban Coalition

CHARLES F. KETTERING, II President, CFK/Ltd

OWEN B. KIERNAN Executive Secretary, National Association of Secondary School Principals

MRS. ELIZABETH D. KOONTZ Director, Women's Bureau, U.S. Department of Labor

GERALD E. KUSLER Principal, Webster Groves, Missouri

WILLIAM S. LITTERICK President, The Educational Records Bureau

RICHARD LONGAKER Committee on Civic Education

EDMUND G. LYONS American Legion

DAVID MALLERY Director of Studies, National Association of Independent Schools

GERALD MARKER Coordinator of Social Studies, Indiana University

RICHARD C. MAXWELL Dean, School of Law, University of California

EDWARD J. MEADE, JR. Program Officer in Charge, Public Education, Ford Foundation

HOWARD D. MEHLINGER Director, High School Curriculum Center in Government, Indiana University

REGINALD MERRIDEW Executive Director, Kiwanis International

JOHN R. MILES Education Manager, Chamber of Commerce of the U.S.

MRS. VIVIAN MONROE Executive Director, Constitutional Rights Foundation

REAR ADM. WILLIAM C. MOTT, U.S.N., RET. Criminal Law Section, American Bar Association, Independent Telephone Association

GEORGE W. O'CONNOR Director, Professional Standards Division, International Association of Chiefs of Police

RICHARD PEARSON President, College Entrance Examination Board

JOHN DE J. PEMBERTON, JR. Executive Director, American Civil Liberties Union

PROFESSOR ART PERL University of Oregon

WENDELL H. PIERCE Executive Director, Education Commission of the States

ROBERT G. PORTER Secretary/Treasurer, American Federation of Teachers

CARY POTTER Executive Secretary, National Association of Independent Schools

MRS. LEON S. PRICE National Congress of Parents and Teachers

CHARLES N. QUIGLEY School of Law, University of California

E. A. RICHTER Director of Information, The Missouri Bar

DONALD F. SANDBERG Program Officer, Public Education, Ford Foundation

GENE L. SCHWILCK Vice President, The Danforth Foundation

MRS. MARY JANE SCRITCHFIELD Association of Classroom Teachers

JAMES B. SHAVER College of Education, Utah State University

MISS ALTHEA T. L. SIMMONS Secretary for Training, National Association for the Advancement of Colored People

RALPH SIU National Institute of Law Enforcement, U.S. Department of Justice

WILLIAM L. SMITH Director, PACE Association

GERALD E. SROUFE Executive Director, National Committee for Support of the Public Schools

JOHN A. STANAVAGE North Central Association of Colleges and Secondary Schools

W. WILLIAMS STEVENS Social Science Education Consortium

JAMES H. STRAUBEL Executive Director, Aerospace Education Foundation

WILLIAM C. SULLIVAN Assistant Director, Federal Bureau of Investigation

PROFESSOR ROBERT S. SUMMERS Association of American Law Schools

THEODORE WALLER President, Grolier Educational Corporation